THE
Bejam
PRACTICAL
FREEZER
HANDBOOK

Jill McWilliam

Above: Quick Béarnaise sauce (left) is made as Hollandaise sauce (right: page 60), substituting wine vinegar for the lemon juice and adding finely chopped shallot and tarragon with the cornflour.
Opposite: Melba sauce (page 61) served over vanilla ice cream.

NOTES

Standard spoon measurements are used in all recipes
1 tablespoon=one 15ml spoon
1 teaspoon=one 5ml spoon
All spoon measures are level.
All eggs are size 3 (standard) unless otherwise stated.
For all recipes, quantities are given in both metric and imperial measures.
Follow either set but not a mixture of both, as they are not interchangeable.
Always preheat the oven or grill to the required temperature and place dishes
in the centre of the oven unless otherwise specified.

Published exclusively for
Bejam
Honeypot Lane,
Stanmore, Middlesex HA7 1LE

by Octopus Books Limited,
59 Grosvenor Street, London W1

First published 1984
© Octopus Books 1984
ISBN 07064 22341

Printed in Hong Kong

CONTENTS

INTRODUCTION

Well over 60% of British households now enjoy the benefits of 'freezer living' and among those remaining, few would not be able to squeeze the few odd packs of frozen 'goodies' into the ice compartment of a refrigerator. Within two decades, our shopping, eating and cooking habits have benefited from this new dimension in preserved food. Today, the convenience of frozen food stored at home is taken for granted . . . less shopping, more variety, cooking when it suits, preserving the garden harvest . . . how did we manage before?

The Bejam Practical Freezer Handbook has been compiled to help you get the best from your freezer. It won't tell you which freezer to buy (the Home Economist at your local Bejam store will do that!) but it is intended to give lots of practical ideas and recipes and to be a reference for when you're 'just not sure'.

Fresh versus frozen

The message of the 80's is 'eating for health', and the British are taking it seriously. Whether it's to lose weight, feel fit or to prevent obesity-related diseases, the quality and quantity of the food we consume is being carefully monitored. So the inevitable question arises 'is frozen food as nutritious as fresh?' The simple answer is yes, but the myths of yesteryear make it difficult for many people to accept. When making any comparisons, the following are worthy of note:

*Fruit and vegetables are harvested at the peak of freshness and frozen within hours, for consumption throughout the following 12 months. Can we always be sure that so called 'fresh' produce has not lost much of its nutritive value during the days – sometimes weeks – of transportation? More vitamins and minerals are lost in prolonged 'harvesting' than in the freezing and storage processes.

*Meat and poultry are matured to prime condition and preserved in this peak state by freezing. Fish is cleaned and frozen at shore-based factories within hours of being caught. Live produce loses nothing in the freezing processes and reaches the domestic freezer in first class condition.

*Frozen foods are, in the main, considerably cheaper than really fresh foods and are also available when needed throughout the year, with little fluctuation in price.

*For the diet-conscious and those with medical dietary needs, the freezer provides a valuable service. Portion-control meals and special food can be difficult and time consuming to prepare. Stored frozen, they are a boon to the 'home dietician'.

Finally, many eminent writers and food nutritionists have endorsed these views over the years. Dr Magnus Pyke has written:

'Most of the fresh vegetables purchased at the greengrocer do not have the same food value as the frozen product. Also frozen foods add variety to the diet and this is one of the fundamental rules of healthy eating.'

And the Long Ashton Research Station at Bristol University has declared: 'Freezing is probably the best method of preservation, as it does preserve the nutritive value of the food without changing its flavour or texture to any great extent.

Freezer work-mate

The only way to organise 'freezer living' is to make your freezer work efficiently. All too often a freezer is used just to store frozen purchases, yet it can provide a variety of services to add to convenience catering and household budgeting. Here are a few well-tried tips:

*Cook and bake when convenient and, wherever possible, adopt the 'eat one, freeze one' method.

*Re-organize the housekeeping and shop monthly – it's time saving and definitely more economical.

*Take advantage of 'special offers' and freeze any real 'bargains'.

*Bread is a must in the freezer and a pack of butter, a carton of milk and some cheese can save the day.

*Shop at a reputable freezer food centre – the range is wider and prices more competitive.

Don't be tempted by unknown brand names – you could be disappointed – and take advantage of 'bulk' packs only when the contents of a smaller pack have won family approval.

*Check prices carefully, especially when bulk buying for home freezing. The same is true with so-called economy packs – the 'investment' must show a substantial saving.

*Complain if foods, frozen or otherwise, do not reach expectations.

Frozen food companies adhere to the strictest specifications of high quality and the public can help to maintain them. No complaint – no action!

*Whenever possible, the storage life of frozen food as stated on the packs should be observed. If the storage life is overrun, however, the food can still be *safely* consumed months later, although texture and flavour may be slightly impaired.

*Be sensible when home-freezing the garden harvest. Freezing a hundred-weight of windfall apples may seem like a money-saving venture, but if they are not used within 12 months (2 apple pies per week) it's a waste of valuable space, time and effort.

*Rotate foods efficiently and re-pack and label as necessary. Defrosting is an excellent opportunity for re-organizing to re-stock.

CARE AND MAINTENANCE

So you've got a freezer. If you're using it correctly, there's no doubt that you're finding it both convenient and economical – in fact it's difficult to imagine how you ever managed without it. Most freezer owners save an average of 10 per cent on their food bills – while the time saved in having a variety of food on tap for all occasions and tastes is incalculable!

Freezing is easy once you get into the swing of things, but to ensure that you get the best out of your freezer, it is important to follow a few basic guidelines. Correct care and maintenance of your freezer are essential so that you don't waste money. Although operating a freezer is simplicity itself, there are a few things which ensure efficient, economical running.

LOCATION

Correct location is important to guard against unnecessarily high running costs and deterioration of the cabinet. A freezer located in a kitchen is convenient, but invariably slightly more expensive to run than if kept in a cooler place such as a cellar, garage or outhouse. If you find it most convenient in the kitchen, try to situate your freezer as far away as possible from the cooker, central heating radiator or other heater. In a cellar, garage or outhouse, guard against possible damp by standing the freezer on a plinth elevated a few inches above the ground for adequate ventilation, and give it a coat of wax car polish from time to time. Damp may cause rusting of the cabinet, but it will not affect the motor unit.

Another precaution worth taking when keeping a freezer outside the main part of the house is to have it fitted with a lock to guard against theft and to prevent young children from climbing inside. Check that wiring is adequately protected if the building is not actually attached to the house and have the wire earthed.

A freezer full of food is extremely heavy, so make sure that the floor it stands on can take the weight. If you keep the freezer upstairs, stand it across the joists to distribute the weight as much as possible.

Remember, too, that the controls should be easily visible so that you can check at a glance that the freezer is running normally – and tape over the plug and socket to safeguard against accidental switching off!

INSURANCE

A well-stocked freezer could contain food worth a lot of money, therefore it is common sense to insure it in the same way as you would any other valuable household item. When buying a new freezer, there will be a guarantee from the manufacturers that they accept responsibility for repairs should the freezer break down during the warranty period, but this does not include food insurance. If a freezer is out of order and waiting for an engineer to call for several days, you stand the risk of losing some or all of its contents. It's not just the monetary value of the food that should concern you – homegrown produce and prepared dishes simply can't be compensated for. Insurance claims don't account for your labours of love, only the face value of the result! So when considering an insurance scheme for your freezer and its contents, shop around for a scheme that offers an emergency service for repairs so that the food can be saved. Freezers and their contents can be covered as part of your general household insurance, but this will not offer emergency repairs, and maintenance contracts are not only expensive and difficult to come by, they rarely operate on a seven-day a week basis.

By far the best insurance schemes available are those offered by freezer food centres at the time you purchase your freezer. These companies are the experts who understand the full significance of a freezer breaking down, so can be relied upon to be efficient and economical. As they are responsible for your insurance claim, it is in their interest to operate a round-the-clock

mobile emergency repair service.

One word of caution with *all* insurance schemes, however – always read the small print very carefully. Check that you are covered for every eventuality, such as accidental switching off or leaving the door/lid open. Also check that you are covered if the freezer breaks down while you are away and cannot give notice within 24 hours.

CLEANING

The outside of the freezer cabinet should be cleaned in exactly the same way as a domestic refrigerator – with a non-abrasive cleaning liquid and warm water. Every six months or so you should clean the fan unit or condenser grille to prevent a build-up of dust. Simply switch off the freezer at the mains, unscrew the inlet grille and then remove the dust carefully with a soft brush or vacuum cleaner hose. Replace the grille and switch on again immediately.

After defrosting (see below) the inside of the cabinet should be washed out in a solution of bicarbonate of soda and warm water (allow 10 ml [2 tsp] soda to 1.2 litres [2 pints] water). Rinse with fresh warm water and dry thoroughly before restocking.

DEFROSTING

This is an essential part of freezer maintenance – a freezer with a build-up of ice will not function efficiently, and will therefore cost more to run. You will need to defrost a chest freezer only once or twice a year, an upright three or four times. In addition, you should regularly scrape away any build-up of ice around the opening of the freezer using a plastic scraper to ensure that the door or lid

will always close properly. It is unnecessary to run stocks down if you are planning to defrost, but choose a reasonably cool day, if possible, to minimize the possibility of food thawing while it is out of the freezer.

Defrosting drill

1 Disconnect freezer from mains.
2 Remove all food, plus baskets, trays and shelves if possible.
3 Ice cream is the food most sensitive to temperature variation, so store this in the ice-making compartment of the refrigerator. Place as much other food as possible in main body of refrigerator. All other items should be stacked in insulated bags, wrapped in blankets or covered with several thicknesses of newspaper and placed in a cold location (outside in winter).
4 Line the bottom of the freezer with towels or several thicknesses of newspaper. Stand one or several bowls of hot water in the freezer, close the door or lid and allow to steam for about 15 minutes.
5 When the ice begins to soften, gently scrape it off with a plastic scraper (never use metal – this will damage the cabinet surface). Work quickly to avoid the ice melting too much and making the job too messy. As the ice falls on to the towels or paper it can be quickly removed.
6 Repeat with fresh hot water if necessary, and continue scraping until the cabinet is entirely clear of ice.
7 Wash the inside of the cabinet, baskets, shelves, etc., with a solution of bicarbonate of soda and warm water (see *Cleaning* above). Dry everything thoroughly, replace the fittings, switch on and re-stock.

WHAT TO DO IN AN EMERGENCY

Make a daily check to see that your freezer is running normally as a matter of course. Regular checks with a thermometer are also a good idea – the reading should be −18°C (0°F). Anything higher than this and the storage life of the food will be affected, whereas running your freezer at a lower temperature is unnecessarily expensive. Note, however, that if you have recently filled the freezer with a lot of unfrozen food this will cause the internal temperature to rise higher and may activate the warning light. Check your thermostat setting regularly and adjust it for seasonal temperature fluctuations.

Breakdowns

If your freezer breaks down, act quickly according to the terms of your insurance policy, but before calling in an engineer, first check that the fault isn't a minor one that you could put right yourself. Check that the door or lid of the freezer hasn't been left open by mistake, or that a fuse hasn't blown.

Power cuts

Although power cuts are not common these days, you should know how to deal with them, just in case! As long as certain precautions are taken, food will be perfectly safe for 24 hours in a freezer which has had its power supply cut off. If prior warning of a power cut is given then so much the better, because there are a few things you can do in advance which will help matters considerably.

1 If possible, move the freezer away from any source of heat.
2 Switch on to fast freeze for an hour or two before the cut is due.
3 Move items which thaw quickly (e.g. ice cream, cakes and baked goods) to the coldest part of the freezer (the bottom of a chest freezer or the back of an upright). Place dense items (e.g. meat) to the top or front.
4 Make sure the freezer is well stacked. If it is not completely full, fill any spaces with crumpled newspaper or boxes – this will help cut down on air circulation.
5 Cover the freezer with blankets.
6 Do not open the freezer again until several hours after the power supply has returned to normal.

REFREEZING

In the unlikely case of an extended power cut, or if your freezer breaks down and cannot be repaired quickly, most foods will thaw in about two days, depending on the weather.

Apart from borrowing space temporarily in neighbours' freezers to store food that is still frozen, what can you do with the rest?

Bread, Cakes and Sweet Pastries

Can be safely refrozen if they do not contain cream or ice cream.

Cooked Dishes

Cannot be refrozen or even recooked and frozen. These should be eaten as soon as possible.

Ice Cream and Cream

Cannot be refrozen. Eat if not completely thawed, otherwise discard.

Raw Fruits

These can be safely refrozen raw. To avoid fruit and juice refreezing as one solid mass, open freeze them on trays first.

Raw Meats, Fish and Vegetables

These should not be refrozen raw. Cook them as quickly as possible, then refreeze as cooked dishes.

FREEZER
KNOW-HOW

Organizing the contents of your freezer should not be overlooked – simply opening the door and pushing packages inside will quickly result in chaos. Sooner or later you won't have a clue what you've got or how long it's been there, so that inevitably food will get forgotten and eventually spoilt through overlong storage.
Try to work out an efficient system from the word go – and stick to it!

LABELLING

Labelling is of utmost importance. Everyone has their own individual system, of course, but all labels should be clear, and you should make sure that they will actually stay on the package during storage. Special freezer labels with adhesive which withstands very low temperatures are a must. Ordinary sticky labels will fall off in the freezer, leaving you with a collection of unmarked parcels – it's surprising how frozen blocks of food all manage to look alike! Always write on labels with a chinagraph or waxed pencil or an oil-based felt tip pen. Any water-based inks or lead-based pencil marks fade during storage. To help with labelling, some freezer bags have labels actually printed on them; you could also have a coding system, using different coloured labels for different kinds of food (e.g. red for meat, blue for fish, green for vegetables and so on). Bags, containers and even freezer ties are available in different colours which will also help with this type of identification. Always state on the label exactly what is inside the package, the quantity, weight and number of servings and the date of freezing. If there is room you can also add thawing or reheating instructions which members of the family might find useful when you are away.

STOCKING AN UPRIGHT FREEZER

Space seems more limited in an upright freezer than in a chest simply because there is less room for manoeuvre. It is therefore vital not to waste space. The average upright freezer will hold 5.5–6.5 kg [12–15 lb] of food per cu ft (the average 10 cu ft family freezer will therefore hold about 68 kg [150 lb] of food). If possible, allow a shelf for different types of food – i.e. fish; fruit and vegetables; and everyday foods like bread, cakes and ice cream. Some upright freezers have compartments in the door, but use this space only for short term storage – a maximum of one month.
Bulk items will most likely need to be split into smaller packages for storage in an upright freezer. Don't forget to label individual packages. Put all items not for immediate use at the back of the shelves to ensure good stock rotation – food should not be stored longer than the maximum recommended storage time if it is to be enjoyed at its best.

Chocolate and cherry bombe (page 57) and Meringue glacé (page 56).

STOCKING A CHEST FREEZER

A chest freezer will hold more per cu ft than an upright – 90 kg [200 lb] of food can be stored in a 10 cu ft chest – but beware that it doesn't become a chaotic jumble! Bulk items can be stored at the bottom, but for everyday smaller packages, dividers and hanging baskets are essential. Plastic carrier bags and cardboard boxes make efficient compartments in the base of the freezer. They can be replaced and reorganized frequently at very little cost. Rotate the stock from the bottom to the top regularly – putting new items in the bottom or fast-freezer compartment and bringing food for immediate use to the top. The fast-freeze compartment is a useful, ready-made section for storing more delicate 'squashable' items like bread and cakes and other decorated goods.

EQUIPMENT

There is a wide range of freezer equipment available in the shops and by mail order, but don't think that all of it is essential. Buy according to your own personal needs and improvise wherever possible to avoid unnecessary expense. Chest freezers are often sold with one or two *hanging baskets* and *dividers* included in the price; extra ones can be bought if you need them, but it is best to have the freezer a while before investing in more.

Blanching baskets and pans are a good investment if you plan to freeze a lot of fresh fruit and vegetables; if you don't, a large saucepan (a pressure cooker pan or preserving pan is ideal) and a large deep-fryer basket will do the job adequately.

Fast-freeze trays are sold specially for open freezing whole or delicate items such as fruit, rosettes of cream, or runner beans, etc., although a baking tray can be used instead.

Extraction of air and proper sealing are all important when you are freezing fresh produce at home, or when you are repacking bulk purchases. There are many kinds of *vacuum pumps* and *heat sealing units* available, but they are expensive. Air can be extracted efficiently with the hands by sucking it out with a drinking straw and sealing with freezer ties can be quite satisfactory.

Two worthwhile investments are a *freezer thermometer* for checking the internal temperature of your freezer and a *freezer knife* for cutting up frozen foods. Freezer knives are far stronger than ordinary kitchen knives, which tend to break when cutting through frozen food. Finally, it's fun, although not exactly indispensable, to have a few novelty items. such as lolly, bombe and decorative ring moulds and hamburger presses, to liven up family meals and snacks!

PACKAGING

As with equipment, it isn't necessary to spend a lot of money on packaging although it is important to realize that correct packaging is vital to protect food during storage in the freezer and thus preserve its quality and life. Incorrect or insufficient packaging means that food will be open to moisture and air, causing dehydration and freezer burn at worst, or damage and cross-flavouring at the very least. Freezer packaging must therefore be strong enough to provide adequate protection, be moisture and vapour proof to exclude all moisture and air, and must, of course, be non-toxic and not taint the food.

The most commonly used packaging materials in the freezer are foil, polythene and cling film. *Freezer foil* is heavy duty, double thickness foil designed for freezer packaging. Ordinary kitchen foil must be used double thickness to provide the same protection. Foil sheeting is ideal for wrapping awkwardly shaped items such as meat with bones, but such packages should be overwrapped in a polythene bag to guard against puncturing. *Foil-trays, basins and other containers* are useful in that food can be frozen and reheated in them and they are re-usable if looked after carefully.

Polythene bags for use in the freezer should be heavy duty (i.e. between 120 and 150 gauge) or they are liable to split at very low temperatures. If using ordinary kitchen bags, use two together to provide adequate protection. Polythene bags are the best all-round packaging for your freezer – they are good for storage in that they take up no more room than the food itself, and they are inexpensive and re-usable. All kinds are available: coloured, boil-in-the-bag and roast-in-the-bag (which can also be used in a microwave oven) and all come with their own ties. Best value for money are bags bought in bulk from freezer centres and mail order companies – shop around for the best prices before you buy.

Rigid polythene containers are essential for items like cakes which need more protection than bags or foil wrapping can give, but they do take up more room in the freezer. Containers with airtight lids are the best quality and will last for many years, so are worthwhile collecting, but you can improvise meanwhile with yogurt, cream, cottage cheese and salad cartons. As these are not airtight and have a tendency to split when handled at low temperatures it is a wise precaution to overwrap them in polythene bags and to use them for short-term storage only. Ice cream containers are ideal for freezer storage, as they are cheap and long-lasting. Collect the 1-litre tubs and 2- and 4-litre boxes.

Cling film is indispensable for close wrapping awkwardly shaped items and for interleaving and wrapping individual slices and portions. Cling film does not offer adequate protection in the freezer on its own, however, but individual items wrapped in cling film can be packed together in one large bag or container. Cling film is not re-usable.

FREEZERPROOF COOKWARE

An efficient and economical method of packing prepared dishes is to freeze them down in the dish in which they have been cooked – virtually any dish which is ovenproof is freezerproof too, although glass should be avoided unless specifically labelled 'freezerproof'. Once frozen solid, the food can be removed from the dish, wrapped in foil or polythene then stored as a neat package. This avoids having to decant food into separate containers, and releases the casserole or dish for day-to-day use while the food is stored in the freezer. To defrost and/or reheat, simply return the food to the original dish.

Microwave cookware is available which is suitable for both freezer storage and cooking in the microwave. However, many kitchen utensils can be used in the microwave and you certainly shouldn't rush out to buy special items until you've taken stock of the contents of your own kitchen cupboards.

STOCKING THE FREEZER

No two families are alike in their shopping habits, likes and dislikes and, above all, in the amount of money they spend on food. Whether you normally shop weekly or less often, you will undoubtedly find it more economical and time-saving to confine your purchase of food for the freezer to monthly or bi-monthly. The convenience and cost-saving soon convince you that this is the best way. Shop around for competitive prices before you buy, bearing in mind that the specialist freezer food centre will have the widest range and variety of pack sizes. Make a list before your shopping trip; although you won't stick to it rigidly, it will help your budget – and too many impulse purchases aren't necessarily a good idea if they end up forgotten in the bottom of the freezer. Also, be cautious at first when buying large packs of unfamiliar items.

For the first few months it may not be possible to make substantial cash savings – this will only come with months of using a well-stocked freezer properly – but the more money you can spend initially the sooner you will reap the benefit financially. About half the initial outlay will be spent on meat, poultry and fish, and the rest spent on vegetables and convenience foods such as burgers, sausages, fish fingers, etc., and a selection of fruits and desserts including ice cream. Account facilities are available at some

freezer food centres at competitive rates, and they are well worth considering as a means of making financial savings from the outset.

MAKE THE MOST OF YOUR FREEZER

Everyone buys a freezer for different reasons, but whatever *your* reasons for owning one, if you use it properly, the quality and choice of all food you eat will improve.

Frozen versus fresh

Some people (usually those who are not freezer owners) regard frozen food as inferior, both from the nutritional and the quality points of view. Of course, this is not true, but you have to remember that the real secret lies in storing only best-quality produce.

The beauty of freezing is that the food is preserved in its natural state and only minimal changes in flavour, texture and nutritional value can be detected on thawing, provided correct preparation and packing methods and storage times are adhered to.

Compared with other methods of food preservation such as bottling, canning, pickling and drying, freezing is far superior. Frozen food looks and tastes closest to fresh, it also retains all its nutrients except a very slight loss of one or two vitamins – but this is minimal compared to loss by other methods of preservation, or in over-long shop storage of so-called 'fresh' foods.

Commercially frozen food

What you may consider to be fresh meat from the butcher may have been delivered to him frozen, then simply thawed before being sold – these days you have no guarantee that what is labelled as 'fresh' actually is so. The

North African lamb (page 50), runner beans, Basic minced beef (page 39) and a selection of herbs, sauces and garnishes being prepared for the freezer.

same applies to fish: most fish you see on the fishmonger's slab has also been frozen and thawed. Far better are packs of frozen meat which you buy in supermarkets and freezer centres which have been 'blast' frozen at extremely low temperatures to preserve the meat's natural quality, and the fish which is actually frozen at sea. Nothing can compare with the flavour and texture of freshly picked home-grown fruit and vegetables, but to ensure maximum freshness, crispness and nutritive value these must be frozen within hours of picking. Most 'fresh' fruit and vegetables don't arrive at the greengrocer or supermarket until two or three days after they have been picked, whereas their counterparts for the freezer are frozen on the farm within hours of picking. Add to this the advantage that fresh produce has a limited season and imported out-of-season fruit and vegetables are expensive, and it is easy to see the advantage of buying frozen. Commercially frozen foods are available all year round at a consistently high quality, with very little fluctuation in price.

Achieving a good balance

To eat fresh in season, frozen out of season, is obviously sound and sensible advice. Use your freezer so that fresh and frozen can complement each other. Frozen produce certainly cuts the monotony of eating only seasonal produce, but it should never be regarded as a substitute for fresh.

BUYING IN LARGE QUANTITIES

Money can definitely be saved by buying large quantities of one particular item, but take care not to overstock. Waste or long storage time in the freezer can cost you money.

Meat

Substantial savings can be made by buying whole or half carcasses of beef, lamb and pork, but check the price per kg (lb) carefully. The quoted price should be on the jointed weight – there is 30 per cent wastage on animal carcasses, so make sure you're not paying for it! Make absolutely sure that the meat is frozen and packed to suit your requirements. On the whole you will probably find it better value for money to buy frozen packs of good-quality cuts which you know and like; this way you can feel confident that nothing is going to be left in the freezer – remember that freezer space is only an asset when fully and sensibly used. Small meat packs from freezer centres are popular with families – these may not be as cheap as buying the whole carcass, but are better value for most families.

Poultry

Frozen poultry is a good buy in that it is convenient and quick to use, especially joints and boneless cubed meat which do not need defrosting before cooking. The 2.5 kg (5 lb) packs of chicken portions are also good value for money but the variety is enormous. Apart from ordinary portions, you can choose whole packs of breasts, thighs, drumsticks or part-boned portions which are good for entertaining, and a variety of 'convenience' type portions and nibbles which are coated in breadcrumbs – perfect for quick family meals. Cuts of turkey, duckling and rabbit are also available in similar packs.

Fish

Unless you live near the coast or other fishing areas, the possibilities of buying freshly caught fish at bargain prices are unlikely. Considerable savings on the normal price per kg (lb) can be made with freezer packs of frozen fish and shellfish. Packs of frozen white, oily and smoked fish are good value in that the whole fish, fillets or steaks are frozen individually so that you can take out as many as you need at a time. Shellfish is available in free-flow packs. The quality is extremely high, because the majority is frozen immediately after catching. Frozen fish is also well worth freezer space in that it is ready-prepared. Convenience-type fish coated in breadcrumbs, batter and sauce, fish cakes and fish fingers, etc., are all good value if bought in larger packs.

Fruit and vegetables

The bulk buying of fresh fruit and vegetables to freeze at home sounds good idea in theory, as is the freezing of homegrown produce; but in practice there are numerous pitfalls. Preparation for the freezer is time-consuming, and you must ensure that you have enough time to deal with the produce immediately – fresh fruit and vegetables in season are extremely perishable and you must work very quickly. When costing out the price per kg (lb) of farm-bought produce, don't forget to take into account the wastage and the time it takes you to get the produce into the freezer, the packaging, and extra electricity costs incurred with the freezing down process. The same goes for homegrown produce: although it is satisfying to take advantage of seasonal gluts from your own garden, these may take up valuable freezer space which could be used for real money savers like special offers from your freezer food centre. Freezer packs of frozen fruits and vegetables compare favourably in price and quality.

Convenience foods

In a sense, all frozen foods are convenience foods in that they are ready-prepared to thaw and/or cook, but prepared foods such as pizzas, flans, pies, part-baked bread, desserts, cakes and ice cream have a place in any well-stocked freezer. They provide quick-and-easy meals and snacks.

HOME-PREPARED DISHES

Freezing dishes that you have prepared yourself at home is far more rewarding and profitable than freezing down the raw ingredients, so you should set aside freezer space to include a selection of home-prepared dishes.

Batch cooking

The freezer phrase 'eat one, freeze one' is sound advice. While you're making a Bolognese sauce for the family supper, for example, it only takes a little while longer to cook twice as much and freeze some away.

Chain cooking

Set aside a time for cooking for the freezer, thus cutting down on labour and fuel costs. The 'chain' is started with the same basic ingredient, which is divided up into portions or family-sized meals and different ingredients added to each; for example, chicken can be made into a variety of casseroles, pastry dishes and curries.

Party cooking

If you are planning a large party your freezer will really come into its own. No more last-minute panics, even if you're catering for a huge crowd, because you can gradually build up a stock of dishes in your freezer, ready-prepared for the big day. This will not only help to distribute the work load more evenly, it will also help with the budget and allow you to take advantage of bargains or seasonal offers.

HOME FREEZING

Freezing down fresh produce at home can be profitable and fun, but this is not the case for all foods. In most cases, the freezing of fresh produce is best left to the professional frozen food companies who have years of experience, plus the benefit of specialist equipment and techniques.

If you do intend to freeze fresh food at home, however, it is important to follow a few simple guidelines. Provided only top-quality produce is used, you are then sure of the best possible results from home freezing.

Fast freezing

This is the real secret to successful freezing. The faster food is frozen, the more chance there is of retaining its natural, fresh quality and texture on thawing, cooking or reheating. During freezing, ice crystals form between the cells of the food; if the food is fast frozen then the ice crystals will be small, if the freezing is slow, then the crystals will be large. Large ice crystals destroy the cell structure of the food – resulting in a disappointing texture and flavour, plus loss of natural juices and valuable nutrients.

A home freezer is only capable of freezing down 10 per cent of its loading capacity in 24 hours; if you exceed this amount, the freezing process will slow down, with poor results. Be aware of the loading capacity of your freezer and always follow the manufacturer's instructions regarding fast freezing. 'Fast freeze' switches have another, perhaps less obvious,

function. By lowering the internal temperature of the cabinet ready for the fresh food to be put inside, they also protect the frozen food that is already in the cabinet, so you should switch on to 'fast freeze' two hours before introducing the food to be frozen. If unfrozen food were put into a freezer running without the use of the 'fast freeze' control, the internal temperature might rise enough to shorten the storage life considerably of the frozen food already in the freezer cabinet.

Use the fast freeze compartment, if available, as it helps keep 'warm' food away from that already frozen.

Not all freezers have a fast freeze compartment, but providing it has a 'fast freeze' switch, it is equipped to do the job. Simply place the food in the coldest part of the freezer, avoiding contact with the already frozen food as far as possible.

If you are freezing large quantities of fresh foods, bear in mind that a maximum loading will take 24 hours to freeze. The fast freeze switch must then be switched off for a further 24 hours, after which more freezing can continue. This is something to consider when harvesting produce.

For freezing down small quantities of fresh food less than 1 kg (2 lb) in weight, the use of the 'fast freeze' control is not necessary – simply place the item(s) in the coldest part of the freezer and keep the freezer closed for a couple of hours.

FREEZING MEAT, POULTRY AND FISH

Meat, poultry and fish can all be fresh frozen satisfactorily, or bought ready frozen from specialist suppliers.

▪ Meat

Some butchers sell whole and half carcasses of beef, veal, lamb and pork which are ready frozen. Beware of seemingly low prices, however, checking exactly what you are getting for your money. Large packs of frozen cuts available at freezer food centres and large supermarkets represent extremely good value in that they are top quality with little or no waste.

When freezing fresh meat make sure that it is properly wrapped to exclude all air and prevent freezer burn (dry, greyish-white patches which appear on meat inadequately wrapped).

▪ Poultry and game

You can freeze fresh poultry and game successfully at home, but it is rarely economically viable. It is best to stock your freezer with commercially frozen quality birds as the prices are usually very keen.

All fresh poultry and game must be hung (if necessary), drawn, plucked or skinned before freezing.

HOW TO FREEZE FRESH MEAT, POULTRY AND GAME

CUT/TYPE	PREPARATION	PACKAGING	STORAGE TIME
Joints	Remove surplus fat and protruding bones, or bone and roll. Tie with string for a neat shape. Skin can be left on pork.	Close wrap individual joints. Pad protruding bones with foil. Overwrap individually in polythene bags.	12 months (beef, veal, lamb) 9 months (pork)
Steaks, chops, cutlets, escalopes, rashers, spareribs	Remove surplus fat. Trim bone ends. Steaks should be no more than 2.5 cm (1 in) thick.	Pad protruding bones. Close wrap individually in cling film then pack in bags.	12 months (beef, veal, lamb) 9 months (pork)
Braising and stewing meat	Remove surplus fat and gristle, etc. Slice or cube.	Pack in polythene bags.	8 months (beef, lamb, pork, veal)
Mince	Only freeze lean meat. Leave loose or shape into servings, adding seasonings to taste.	Pack loose mince in usable quantities in polythene bags. Open freeze shaped mince, then pack in bags.	6 months
Offal (brains, kidneys, hearts, liver)	Clean. Remove fat, gristle, etc. Leave whole, slice or cube.	Pack whole items and slices in polythene bags, interleaving with foil/cling film.	6 months

Never stuff whole birds before freezing as the stuffing may prevent thawing out and cooking thoroughly. Double-wrap poultry and game as the flesh of birds is particularly prone to freezer burn.

Giblets must be frozen separately because their storage life is shorter.

Fresh fish and shellfish

Fish and shellfish for freezing must be absolutely fresh – the process is therefore best left to frozen food companies who have the facilities to freeze immediately after catching.

Do not freeze the 'fresh fish' from a wet fishmonger; it may well be more than 24 hours old or already thawed. Fish are generally gutted before freezing to prevent discoloration of the flesh, and divided into fillets and steaks for convenience, but in the case of a freshwater fish, such as a salmon, you may want to keep it whole for presentation. The best method of freezing a whole fish is ice glazing: freeze unwrapped, then dip in ice-cold water and return to the freezer until a thin film of ice forms around the fish. Repeat 3 or 4 times until a 3 mm (⅛ inch) layer of ice has built up, then wrap in cling film and overwrap in a polythene bag.

HOW TO FREEZE FRESH MEAT, POULTRY AND GAME

CUT/TYPE	PREPARATION	PACKAGING	STORAGE TIME
Sausages, sausagemeat	Must be freshly made, not fatty or highly spiced.	Open freeze sausages until solid then pack together in bags. Pack sausagemeat in bags.	6 months
Bacon (rashers and joints)	Only freeze very fresh mild-cured bacon. Vacuum-packed rashers are best.	Pad protruding bones. Close wrap individually and overwrap in bags. Double wrap rashers and wrap vacuum packs in bags.	6 months
Whole birds	Remove giblets, separate liver. Wash inside and out, dry, then truss as necessary.	Pad protruding bones. Wrap individually in foil/cling film. Overwrap in bags. Pack giblets in bags.	12 months (chicken, poussin, turkey) 6 months (duck, goose, game birds) 6 months (giblets)
Halves, portions, joints	Remove protruding bone ends. Wash and dry.	Close wrap individual pieces in foil, then pack in bags.	As for Whole birds above
Furred game (e.g. hare, rabbit, venison)	Freeze only young animals. Prepare as necessary, leaving small animals whole. Cut large into joints.	Close wrap individually in cling film (first padding protruding bones), then pack in bags.	12 months (venison) 6 months (hare, rabbit)

FREEZING FRESH VEGETABLES

Buying vegetables for freezing from pick-your-own farms is usually cheaper and fresher than the local greengrocer or market. It is far more rewarding, of course, to grow your own – you can harvest and freeze them in the shortest possible time without additional transport costs. However, commercially frozen vegetables are top quality, and cheaper than any home-frozen vegetables so there aren't any great savings to be made by freezing vegetables at home.

Vegetables to be frozen at home *must* be freshly harvested when they are in peak condition, young and tender. Blanching is usually necessary to promote long storage life in the freezer, and since this is a laborious task, make sure you set aside enough time to do it. However, some vegetables will freeze successfully for a period of months without blanching. *Don't* be tempted to pick more vegetables than you can reasonably expect to cope with or they will lose their freshness before you have got them in the freezer, so defeating the object of the exercise. When growing for freezing, choose varieties that are recommended – most seed packets and nurseries now give this information.

The unfreezables

Some vegetables do not freeze successfully because of their high water content, others such as cabbage and whole potatoes are bulky, and because they are available all year round, are simply not worth taking up valuable freezer space. Most salad vegetables – chicory, cucumber, endive, lettuce, watercress, etc. – go limp and soggy in the freezer; they are best frozen as part of a cooked dish such as soup or sauce. Vegetables such as celery, onions, tomatoes and peppers lose their crispness and texture in the freezer and cannot be eaten raw after thawing, but they can be frozen for future use in cooking.

Avocados, aubergines and mushrooms tend to discolour in the freezer and lose their texture, giving disappointing results unless part of made-up dishes. The vegetables listed in the chart on the next page are those that warrant freezer space.

Blanching

Blanching inactivates enzymes present in the vegetables which would otherwise continue to work in the freezer and cause the vegetables to lose texture, colour, flavour and nutritional value. For short-term storage, blanching can be omitted in the case of the following vegetables: peas, peppers, spinach, sweetcorn and tomatoes. As it is not economical use of freezer space to store more than 2–3 months' supply of vegetables it could be argued that blanching is totally unnecessary. In fact it is a matter of personal choice.

Blanching is time-consuming because you can only blanch 500 g [1 lb] of vegetables at a time, but it is not difficult – and remember that the blanching water can be used as many as 6 or 7 times before it needs changing, which saves time and helps retain vitamin C content.

How to blanch

1 Bring a large pan containing 4 litres [7 pints] of water to the boil.
2 Place 500 g [1 lb] prepared vegetables in the blanching basket and immerse in the water.
3 Bring the water back to the boil within 1 minute, then calculate the blanching time from this moment. Times are given overleaf.
4 Time very carefully and remove the basket immediately, immersing it in a bowl of iced water for the same length of time as blanching.
5 Drain well, pat dry with kitchen paper and pack immediately.

Storage times

Storage times are not given in the chart because 2–3 months is the maximum time to store vegetables economically, although most vegetables will keep for up to 12 months.

HOW TO FREEZE FRESH VEGETABLES

VEGETABLE	PREPARATION	BLANCHING TIME (in minutes)	PACKAGING
Asparagus	Only freeze very young and tender stems. Grade according to thickness. Wash and tie in bundles.	2–4 according to thickness of stems.	Pack in rigid containers (bags do not provide sufficient protection).
Beans, broad	Freeze very young beans in pods, or pod and grade by size.	2–3	Open freeze until solid, then pack free-flow in bags.
Beans, French	Beans should snap cleanly and not be stringy. Cut off ends.	1–2	Pack in bags. Or open freeze and pack free-flowing.
Beans, runner	Top and tail and string, if necessary. Slice into 2.5 cm (1 inch) pieces.	1–2	As French beans above.
Broccoli/Cauliflower	Choose compact heads. Divide into short florets, removing woody stalks. Wash in salted water.	3	Open freeze until solid. Pack broccoli in rigid containers, alternating heads and stalks. Pack cauliflower in bags.
Brussels sprouts	Only freeze small sprouts with tight, compact heads. Remove outer leaves. Cut a cross in stalk.	3	Open freeze until solid, then pack free-flow in polythene bags.
Carrots	Leave small carrots whole, removing green tops. Rub off skins after blanching.	4 (whole) 2 (sliced/diced)	Open freeze until solid. Pack in polythene bags.
Celery	Too limp after thawing to be eaten raw, but prepare for future use in cooking – cut stalks into chunks.	3	Open freeze until solid. Pack in usable quantities in polythene bags.
Courgettes	Only freeze the smallest courgettes.	2 (whole) 1 (sliced)	As Brussels sprouts above.
Leeks	Cut off roots and green tops. Wash thoroughly.	4 (whole) 3 (sliced/chopped)	As Celery above.

HOW TO FREEZE FRESH VEGETABLES

VEGETABLE	PREPARATION	BLANCHING TIME (in minutes)	PACKAGING
Onions	Too watery to be used raw after thawing, but can be used in cooking. Peel. Leave small (pickling) onions whole. Slice or chop large onions.	2 (whole) 1 (sliced/chopped)	Open freeze whole or sliced onions until solid then pack free-flow in bags. Double wrap all onion packs to prevent cross-flavouring.
Parsnips, Swedes and Turnips	Trim and peel. Leave whole, slice or dice.	4 (whole) 2 (sliced)	As Celery.
Peas (incl mange-touts)	Only freeze the very youngest, tiny peas. Pod. Top and tail mange-touts.	1 (peas and mange-touts)	As Brussels sprouts.
Peppers (capsicums)	Too limp to be eaten raw after thawing, but prepare for future use in cooking.	3 (whole/halved) 2 (sliced/diced)	As Brussels sprouts.
Potatoes, new	Only small, very new potatoes are worth freezing. Scrape and cook until almost tender. Cool.	—	As Celery.
Potatoes, old	Only suitable for freezing as chips, croquettes or duchesse potatoes.	—	As Brussels sprouts. Pack frozen duchesse potatoes in rigid containers, separating layers with foil.
Spinach	Pick over carefully in iced water, removing discoloured leaves and coarse stalks. Or cook until just tender, then purée and cool.	2 (whole leaves)	Leaf spinach as Celery. Pack purée in usable quantities in rigid containers.
Sweetcorn	Choose tender (not over-ripe) cobs. Remove husks and silks. Cut kernels off cobs after blanching if wished.	4–8 (according to size of cob)	Ensure cobs are cold in centre before packing together in polythene bags. Pack kernels as Brussels sprouts.
Tomatoes	Leave whole or cut in half. Or make into juice/purée/sauce/soup. Cool.	—	Pack whole and half tomatoes in bags. Pack , juice, etc., in rigid containers.

FREEZING FRESH FRUIT

Freezing is by far the quickest method of preserving fruit, which is a real boon in times of glut. Not all fruits are suitable for freezing in their natural state, however. Some juicy fruits are best packed with sugar, whereas firm-textured stone fruits which discolour easily are most successful frozen in a sugar syrup. Fruits with a high water content (e.g. strawberries) are best crushed or puréed before being frozen. Bananas go black and lose their texture, so are virtually unfreezable unless mashed into an ice cream or cheesecake mixture.

Freshness and quality are all-important when freezing fruit, so too is speed. Ideally, fruit should be frozen within 2 hours of harvesting, so pick and freeze according to the time available.

Only freeze perfect fruit. Over-ripe fruits which are soft and juicy can be frozen in juice or purée form, but make sure they have no trace of damage or mould. Avoid using utensils and pans made of galvanized iron, copper or brass as these may taint the flavour of the fruit and cause discoloration. For the same reason, always remove stones and pips.

Methods of freezing fruit

Dry and free-flow packs are only suitable for fruits which have a high vitamin C content and do not discolour easily. Blackberries, currants, cherries, gooseberries and raspberries and the most suitable. Don't bother to remove stalks from currants – these can be rubbed off the frozen fruit in a matter of seconds. Either pack in usable quantities in polythene bags or open freeze on trays until solid, then pack 'free-flow' in bags.

Dry sugar packs are best for all soft, juicy fruits, except apricots, peaches and pears, which discolour easily and need to be packed in a sugar syrup. Prepare the fruit as necessary and pack fruit in rigid containers, sprinkling each layer of fruit with caster sugar. Allow 100–175 g [4–6 oz] sugar for every 500 g [1 lb] fruit, according to taste. Leave 2 cm (¾ inch] headspace before sealing with the lid, to allow room for expansion.

Sugar syrup packs are for hard, non-juicy fruits and those which discolour easily such as apricots and pears. The syrup needs to be chilled before use, so it is a good idea to make up the quantity you need earlier, allowing fruit to be prepared straight into it.

As a general guide, you will need 300 ml [½ pint] syrup for every 500 g [1 lb] fruit. Strengths of sugar syrup vary according to the type of fruit (and personal taste), but a medium sugar syrup – 350 g [12 oz] sugar to 600 ml [1 pint] water – is mostly used. To avoid discoloration, add ¼ tsp ascorbic acid powder or 1 tsp lemon juice, to every 600 ml [1 pint] of syrup.

Dissolve the sugar over gentle heat in a heavy pan, then boil without stirring for 2 minutes. Leave to cool, then chill overnight. Pack fruit and syrup in rigid containers, leaving 2 cm [¾ inch] headspace. As an extra safeguard against discoloration, place a piece of crumpled Cellophane or greaseproof paper on top of the fruit to help keep it submerged. Seal immediately.

Fruit purées and juices are less bulky to store than whole fruit or slices. Sieve raw or cooked fruit, adding sugar according to taste and future use.

Storage time

Most fruits can be stored satisfactorily for 8–10 months, after which time discoloration may occur.

HOW TO FREEZE FRESH FRUIT

FRUIT	PREPARATION	PACKAGING	STORAGE TIME
Apples (only worth freezing cooking apples)	Peel and core. Slice or cut into rings. Or cook to a purée, sweetened according to use.	Pack slices/rings in usable quantities in polythene bags. Pack cold purée in rigid containers.	8–10 months uncooked 8 months puréed
Apricots/peaches	Only freeze firm fruit. Scald 10–15 seconds and then skin. Halve or slice, stone and brush with lemon juice.	Pack in medium sugar syrup in rigid containers.	8–10 months
Berries (bilberries, blackberries, elderberries, gooseberries, loganberries, raspberries, strawberries) and currants (black, red, white)	Pick over fruit. Do not wash. Leave perfect fruits (except strawberries) whole. Gooseberries can also be poached with water and sugar, or cooked to a purée. Raspberries and currants can also be puréed and sieved. Strawberries are best crushed, or puréed.	Dry pack whole fruit in polythene bags, free-flow if wished. Pack cold poached, crushed and puréed fruit in rigid containers.	10 months
Cherries	Remove stalks and stones.	Dry pack in bags. Or pack in medium sugar syrup in rigid containers.	10 months
Citrus fruit	Peel and divide into segments or slice into rings (frozen lemon slices are convenient for drinks, garnishing and decorating).	Dry pack, dry sugar pack segments/slices or pack in medium sugar syrup in rigid containers, according to future use.	10 months
Pears (only worth freezing cooking pears or very firm dessert pears)	Peel, halve and core. Quarter if wished. Brush flesh with lemon juice. Can also be poached with water and sugar.	Pack halves/quarters in medium sugar syrup in rigid containers. Pack poached fruit in cold poaching liquid.	8–10 months
Plums, damsons and greengages	Wash, but do not skin. Halve and remove stones. Whole damsons can be poached and puréed.	Pack in medium sugar syrup in rigid containers. Pack cold damson purée in rigid containers.	10 months
Rhubarb	Wash, cut into 2.5 cm [1 in] lengths.	Dry sugar pack in polythene bags.	10 months

FREEZING FRESH DAIRY PRODUCE

The advantage of freezing dairy produce is convenience rather than economy. But it is not worth too much freezer space. A packet or two of butter and cheese are useful standbys if you run out, and a bag of free-flow grated cheese is convenient to use when you are in a hurry. Cream is a 'must' in the freezer, but buy ready frozen in pieces. It is ready to thaw and serve in the quantities you require and can be dropped frozen into a soup or casserole to add richness just before serving. It's also a good idea to keep some whipped cream or piped cream rosettes to add a little luxury to an everyday dessert, cake or pastry, or last-minute entertaining.

Milk is not worth freezing unless you live in a remote country district where fresh supplies are not delivered on a regular basis. Never freeze milk in bottles as they may shatter at such a low temperature, but a carton of milk is a useful standby.

Eggs cannot be frozen whole or hard-boiled, but if you have leftover yolks or whites they can be frozen to be incorporated in cooked dishes.

Homemade ice cream is expensive to make and time-consuming and is hardly worthwhile with such a wide variety

HOW TO FREEZE DAIRY PRODUCE

DAIRY PRODUCE	PREPARATION	PACKAGING	STORAGE TIME
Butter	Must be very fresh, so freeze as soon as possible.	Keep in original wrapper, overwrap in polythene bag.	6 months (unsalted) 3 months (salted)
Cheese, hard	Divide into usable quantities. Grate if wished, according to future use.	Keep in original wrappers if possible and overwrap in polythene bags. If cut, close wrap in foil or cling film then overwrap in bag. Pack grated cheese in bags.	3–4 months
Cheese, soft and cream	Freeze only mature soft cheeses. Cream cheeses must have at least 40 per cent butterfat content.	Pack soft cheeses as for hard above. Pack cream cheeses in usable quantities in rigid containers.	As for hard cheese above
Cream	Only freeze very fresh cream with at least 40 per cent butterfat. Chill, then whip with 1 teaspoon sugar per 150 ml (¼ pint). Pipe into rosettes on non-stick trays.	Pack whipped cream in usable quantities in rigid containers. Open freeze rosettes until solid, then pack in containers interleaved with foil.	3 months

of commercially prepared ice cream available at very competitive prices. Commercially made fruit yogurts can be frozen with reasonable results – it is best to stick to commercially frozen yogurts, which are available in family packs at freezer food centres.

FREEZING HOME-PREPARED DISHES AND BAKED GOODS

Cooking for the freezer can be profitable and satisfying; you can either set aside time specifically for it (see Batch and Chain Cooking – page 000) or simply make one or two extras when preparing ordinary, everyday meals. This way you can very quickly build up a stock of prepared dishes in the freezer, so that when you're too busy to cook or not at home there will always be a nutritious homemade dish on hand. Always freeze cooked dishes in convenient-sized amounts to suit your family's needs, to avoid wastage. The foods listed in the chart on this page are the ones most suited to freezing, but don't look on this as a definitive list. It isn't necessary to use only recipes from freezer books; with a few exceptions such as clear jellies and blancmanges, dishes containing mayonnaise, aspic or hard-boiled eggs, most dishes found in ordinary recipe books will freeze satisfactorily.

HOW TO FREEZE DAIRY PRODUCE

DAIRY PRODUCE	PREPARATION	PACKAGING	STORAGE TIME
Eggs	Eggs in shells and hard-boiled eggs will not freeze. Lightly beat whole eggs with ½ tsp salt or 1 tsp sugar (according to future use) for every 3 eggs. Freeze egg yolks beaten with ¼ tsp salt or 1 tsp sugar for every 3 yolks. Freeze egg whites as they are, without beating or additions.	Pack beaten whole eggs, yolks and whites in usable quantities in rigid containers.	6 months
Ice cream, homemade	Divide into usable quantities, individual desserts, etc.	Pack in rigid containers.	3 months
Milk	Only freeze homogenized milk.	Decant from bottles into rigid containers.	1 month
Yogurt	Freeze only commercially prepared yogurts.	Overwrap original cartons in polythene bags.	6 weeks

HOW TO FREEZE HOME-PREPARED DISHES

DISH	PREPARATION	PACKAGING	STORAGE TIME
Casseroles, stews and baked dishes (e.g. lasagne, moussaka, shepherd's pie)	Cook in the usual way until meat is just tender, avoiding too much garlic, heavy seasoning and wine. Do not thicken. Cool. Freeze large quantities in one solid block (e.g. in a roasting tin).	Open freeze in casserole lined with large sheet of foil until solid, then turn out, wrap in foil, then overwrap in polythene bag. Open freeze block until just firm, then cut into neat portions and wrap each in foil. Pack portions in bags.	3 months
Meringues	Make in the usual way and cool. Fill with cream if wished.	Open freeze on trays until solid, then pack carefully in rigid containers. Separate each meringue with cardboard or several thicknesses of foil to prevent breakages.	3 months
Mousses and soufflés, cold (sweet and savoury)	Make according to individual recipe in the usual way (gelatine freezes well).	Cover bowl with foil then overwrap in a polythene bag.	2 months (if set with gelatine) 1 month (if set with just cream and eggs)
Puddings	Prepare charlottes, crumbles, sponges, etc., in foil containers. Freeze cooked or uncooked.	Wrap in foil containers in polythene bags.	3 months
Sauces (e.g. apple, béchamel, bolognese, bread, cheese, chocolate, fruit, white)	Make in bulk, then divide into usable quantities.	Pack in usable quantities in rigid containers.	3 months
Soups	Make in the usual way but do not overseason or thicken. Skim off all fat after cooling.	Pack in usable quantities in rigid containers.	3 months
Stock	Make in the usual way, boiling to reduce if freezer space is limited. Skim off all fat after cooling	Pack in usable quantities in rigid containers. Freeze concentrated stock in ice cube trays until solid, then pack in bags.	3 months

HOW TO FREEZE BAKED GOODS

BAKED GOODS	PREPARATION	PACKAGING	STORAGE TIME
Biscuits, homemade	Form unbaked dough into long rolls, or pipe/shape on to trays. Cooked biscuits should have a high fat content. Cool before freezing.	Wrap rolls in foil/cling film, then overwrap in polythene bags. Open freeze shapes until solid, then pack in rigid containers, interleaving with foil.	6 months
Bread, baked (commercial and homemade – brown and white)	Only freeze very fresh loaves and rolls, preferably on the day of baking and without too much crust. Sliced bread can be successfully frozen. Freezer centres stock a wide selection of part- and wholly-baked frozen bread.	Wrap loaves individually in foil then overwrap in polythene bags. Pack rolls in rigid containers, interleaving layers with foil. Leave sliced bread in original wrappings, overwrap.	6 months (plain white and brown, and sliced) 3 months (enriched doughs) 3–7 days (crusty loaves, e.g. French sticks and viennas) 3 months (part- and wholly-baked bread)
Bread, unbaked (commercial and homemade – brown and white)	Increase yeast by 50 per cent. Make dough, knead then freeze immediately. Or knock back after first rising and freeze.	Pack dough in a large greased polythene bag, to allow room for rising/proving on thawing.	1 month
Cakes	Freeze as soon as possible after cooling. Avoid using large quantities of spices, synthetic flavourings, jam fillings, glacé, royal, boiled and fondant icings and decorations such as nuts, fruit, etc. Cut large cakes into slices if wished.	Wrap undecorated cakes in cling film/foil then overwrap in polythene bags. Open freeze fancy, decorated and iced cakes until solid, then pack in rigid containers. Pack small cakes/slices in rigid containers, interleaving with foil.	10 months (fat-free sponges) 4 months (plain and fruit cakes) 3 months (fancy/decorated/iced) 2 months (with fresh cream fillings/toppings).
Pastry and pastry-based dishes	Shape uncooked blocks of pastry in usable quantities. Make pies, quiches, tarts, etc., in foil dishes or in foil-lined plates or dishes and leave uncooked, or bake and cool.	Wrap blocks of pastry individually in cling film/foil, then pack together in bags. Open freeze made-up dishes until solid, wrap in foil/cling film then overwrap in bags.	1–3 months (according to fillings in made-up dishes)
Pizza	Make according to usual recipe. Leave uncooked or bake and cool.	Open freeze on large sheet of foil until solid, then wrap in foil and overwrap in bags.	1 month

THAWING
FROZEN FOOD

Some foods are best thawed before cooking and some not, and it's really a matter of getting to know the food you store in the freezer and learning from experience. The charts in this chapter give instructions for cooking from frozen or thawing. There are also a few general guidelines which are worth remembering.

1 Cooking from frozen preserves the juices which are naturally present in food, therefore many foods such as vegetables and fish actually benefit from being cooked this way. If instructions are given for cooking from frozen, then always follow these for best results.

2 Dense foods such as meat should be thawed to ensure accurate cooking. Even with the use of a meat thermometer, it is difficult to tell whether the meat in the centre of a large joint is cooked to the right degree.

3 In general, food to be thawed should be placed in the refrigerator. This ensures that ice crystals break down slowly and do not rupture the cell walls of the food. 'Drip' from food will be kept to an absolute minimum if thawed at refrigerator temperature. The only exceptions to this rule are cooked foods and prepared dishes which do not suffer from 'drip' and can therefore be thawed at room temperature for quickness.

4 Avoid thawing in cold water – this only accelerates 'drip'. Never thaw in warm water.

MEAT

Thawing is recommended prior to cooking for two reasons:
1 It is easier to cook meat more accurately.
2 Cooking from frozen necessitates longer cooking, which in turn can cause dryness.

Be sure to thaw meat properly in order to achieve the most tender, juicy results on cooking. Remove the meat from its wrapping and stand it on a dish or plate with a lip so that the 'drip' can be caught. Cover the meat with cling film and place it in the refrigerator to ensure slow thawing and thus minimal loss of natural juices. Leave small cuts of meat and joints to thaw for 24 hours, larger joints for as long as 36–48 hours. Never throw away the 'drip' which collects during thawing; use it to baste, or as part of a sauce or gravy.

POULTRY & GAME

It is essential to thaw whole birds before cooking, otherwise it is very difficult to tell whether the meat is cooked right through to the centre or not – the outer flesh may be cooked to perfection, but the interior carcass and flesh may still be frozen.

Thaw in the refrigerator for the best results – or in cold water in emergencies. All poultry and game portions will cook satisfactorily from frozen as there is no carcass barrier to prevent heat penetration.

HOW TO THAW/COOK UNCOOKED FROZEN FOODS

FROZEN PRODUCE	THAWING	COOKING FROM FROZEN	THAWING BY MICROWAVE
Meat, joints	Unwrap, then place on dish or plate. Cover with cling film and thaw in refrigerator for 24 hours (small joints), 36–48 hours (larger joints).	Cook slowly in a moderate oven and test for thorough cooking with a meat thermometer.	Defrost 2 min, stand 2 min per 450 g (1 lb); repeat twice and stand extra 10 min (covered) before cooking. Turn over after first cycle.
Meat, steak and chops, etc.	Unwrap, then place on dish or plate. Cover with foil and thaw in refrigerator overnight, at room temperature 6–8 hours.	Grill or fry, adding 5 minutes to the cooking time.	Defrost 2 min, stand 2 min per 450 g (1 lb); repeat and stand extra 2 min (covered) before cooking. Turn over and separate chops after first cycle.
Meat, stewing and braising cuts, mince	Unwrap, then place on dish or plate. Cover with foil and thaw in refrigerator overnight, or partially thaw for 4 hours, then fry in oil and butter before proceeding with recipe.	If meat is to be fried before use in stews and pies, etc., fry gently in hot fat until thawed and browned. Alternatively, simmer meat in hot stock until separated.	Place in a dish covered with pierced clingfilm. Defrost 2 min, stand 2 min per 450 g (1 lb); repeat and stand extra 2–8 min (covered) before cooking. Rearrange after each cycle.
Offal/sausages/ sausagemeat	Thaw offal as stewing meat above. Thaw sausagemeat in refrigerator 4–6 hours.	Cook straight from frozen. Fry in oil or fat/brush with oil or melted fat and grill for 20 minutes, using low heat.	Defrost 2 min, stand 2 min per 450 g (1 lb); repeat and stand extra 5 min (covered) before cooking. Separate after first cycle.
Burgers	Not recommended.	Fry in melted fat over low heat for about 15 minutes or according to packet instructions.	Not recommended.
Bacon (knuckle/ collar/forehock) and gammon, joints	If salty, soak frozen joints 24 hrs in cold water. Drain and cook according to individual recipes, allowing 20–25 minutes per lb for gammon, 35–45 minutes for bacon (depending on type of cut).	Place frozen joint in pan of cold water and bring slowly to boil. Drain and cook according to individual recipes.	Place in dish and cover with pierced clingfilm. Defrost 2 min, stand 2 min per 450 g (1 lb); repeat twice and stand extra 5–10 min (covered) before cooking.

HOW TO THAW/COOK UNCOOKED FROZEN FOODS

FROZEN PRODUCE	THAWING	COOKING FROM FROZEN	THAWING BY MICROWAVE
Bacon rashers	Thaw small packs of rashers in refrigerator, then separate and cook as fresh.	Not possible unless rashers are separated.	Defrost 2 min, stand 2 min; repeat and stand extra 5 min (covered) before cooking.
Pizza	Not recommended.	Bake in a 200°C (400°F) Gas Mark 6 oven for 20 minutes or grill according to packet instructions.	Cook straight from frozen.
Poultry and game, whole birds	Thaw in refrigerator: 12–24 hrs (under 3 lb) 24–36 hrs (3–5 lb) 2–3 days (under 8 lb) 3–4 days (8–14 lb) 4–5 days (14–20 lb) 5–6 days (over 20 lb)	Not recommended.	Defrost 2 min, stand 2 min per 450 g (1 lb); repeat twice, remove giblets and stand extra 10 min (covered) before cooking. Turn after each cycle.
Poultry and game, portions and joints, etc.	Not necessary but can be thawed if preferred. Thaw 6–8 hours in refrigerator.	Fry or grill in butter, basting. Test by piercing with a skewer – juice should be creamy, not red.	Place thinnest parts at centre. Defrost as whole birds.
Fish and shellfish	Not recommended, but if to be incorporated into a made-up dish, can be thawed overnight in refrigerator. Unwrap whole fish and thaw loosely covered in refrigerator for up to 12 hours. Thaw prawns 5–6 hours in refrigerator, 1½–2½ hours at room temperature. Rinse and dry before use.	Fry or grill over low heat, basting frequently. Add ⅓ to normal cooking time.	Cover prawns in pierced clingfilm. Defrost 2 min, stand 2 min plus an extra 5–10 min (covered) before cooking. Cook whole fish, fillets, steaks and shellfish straight from frozen.
Vegetables	Not recommended.	Plunge into boiling salted water, allowing 2.5 cm (1 inch) water for every 225 g (½ lb).	Cook straight from frozen.
Fruit	To serve raw/cold, thaw in unopened containers approx 3 hrs in refrigerator.	Poach/stew/use in made-up dishes.	Defrost 2 min, stand 2 min per 450 g (1 lb); repeat and stand extra 5 min.

FISH & SHELLFISH

It is advisable to cook all fish from frozen, apart from very large whole fish where body cavities may prevent thorough cooking.

Shellfish coated in an ice glaze should have this thawed off prior to use.

FRUIT

As most fruits have a high water content, they tend to go limp on thawing. For the best results, therefore, most frozen fruits are best used for cooking or in made-up desserts, in which case they should be cooked from frozen to avoid overcooking. Check first whether the fruit has been frozen with sugar or in a sugar syrup or not. Soft juicy fruits such as raspberries and strawberries are best served slightly iced so that they retain their shape as much as possible. All fruits which tend to discolour quickly on exposure to air (e.g. pears and apricots) should be thawed in their unopened containers in the refrigerator and served promptly.

VEGETABLES

To get the best results from vegetables, cook from frozen for the minimum amount of time. This will guard against overcooking which gives soggy, unappetising vegetables with much of their nutritive value lost. To be enjoyed at their best, vegetables should be crisp and full of flavour, and frozen vegetables will taste as good as fresh if cooking instructions are carefully followed. This is especially important if they have been blanched.

Vegetable Lasagne (page 73).

HOW TO THAW DAIRY PRODUCE

DAIRY PRODUCE	THAWING	COOKING FROM FROZEN	THAWING BY MICROWAVE
Butter	Remove overwrapping. Thaw 2 hrs at room temperature.	Can be sliced using a strong (freezer) knife and used for melting/ cooking.	Remove overwrapping. Defrost 1½–2 min, stand 5 min.
Cheese	Thaw in wrappings overnight in refrigerator. Soft cheeses need to 'come to' at room temperature before serving. Cream cheeses may need stirring until they are smooth.	Grated cheese remains free-flow and can be used frozen in cooked dishes.	Not recommended for most cheeses. For cream cheese, remove foil wrap, place on paper towel, defrost 1–1½ min, stand 10–15 min.
Cream	Thaw cream pieces 1–2 hours. Whisk before use. Place piped rosettes on cakes. etc., and thaw for approx 30 mins at room temperature.	Small blocks of frozen cream can be dropped into hot sauces/soups/ casseroles, etc. Stir to dissolve.	Remove lid and defrost 1–2 min, stand 10 min.
Eggs	Transfer whole eggs/ yolks/whites to a bowl and leave 1 hr at room temperature. Beat lightly before use.	N/A	Not recommended.
Ice cream	Never thaw or refreeze after thawing. Hard ice cream can be softened for 30 minutes in refrigerator before serving if necessary.	N/A	N/A
Milk	Thaw in container overnight in refrigerator. If milk shows signs of curdling, bring to boil, cool and use quickly.	N/A	Not recommended.
Yogurt	Thaw in original container overnight in refrigerator. Stir before use.	N/A	Not recommended.

HOW TO THAW OR COOK PREPARED DISHES

DISH	THAWING	COOKING FROM FROZEN	THAWING BY MICROWAVE
Bread and bread dough	Thaw whole loaves in wrapping approx 3 hrs at room temperature, buns and rolls 1½ hrs.	Unrisen dough: reseal bag to allow room for rising. Allow 5 hrs at room temperature, overnight in refrigerator. Risen dough: remove from bag. Toast sliced bread from frozen.	Wrap in clingfilm. Defrost whole loaves 4 min, stand 8 min; defrost buns and rolls 1 min.
Cakes	Leave plain cakes in wrappings; Unwrap iced and decorated cakes. Thaw small cakes 1–2 hrs at room temperature, large cakes 3–4 hours, iced and fruit cakes up to 6 hrs.	N/A	Remove wrappings. Defrost small cakes 1–1½ min; large plain cakes 2½ min, stand 10 min; fruitcakes 4 min, stand 10 min.
Casseroles/stews/lasagne/etc.	Not necessary, but can be thawed if preferred. Thaw 6–8 hrs at room temperature, 24 hrs in refrigerator.	Unwrap and return to original dish/casserole/etc. Reheat in preheated 180°C (350°F) Gas 4 oven for approx 2 hrs.	Defrost 15–20 min, stand 20 min per 450 g (1 lb). Reheat as required.
Fish dishes (e.g. fish cakes/mousses/kedgeree)	Thaw mousses overnight in refrigerator. Thaw fish dishes in sauce 3–4 hrs at room temperature then reheat in 180°C (350°F) Gas 4 oven.	Fry or grill fish cakes/fingers, basting frequently. Reheat kedgeree, etc., in preheated 180°C (350°F) Gas 4 oven 30–40 minutes.	Defrost 2–3 min, stand 5 min per 450 g (1 lb). Reheat as required.
Pastry-based dishes (savoury and sweet pies/tarts/flans, etc.)	Not recommended for uncooked frozen items. Cooked frozen items should be thawed 2–4 hrs at room temperature. If required, reheat in preheated 180°C (350°F) Gas 4 oven for approx 10 mins.	Bake uncooked items in preheated 220°C (425°F) Gas 7 oven 35–45 mins. Glaze after 15 minutes and cover to avoid overbrowning. Large savoury pies should be cooked an extra 15–30 mins at reduced temperature.	Defrost savoury pies 5–7 min, stand 5 min; sweet pies 1–2 min, stand 5 min.
Soups/sauces/stocks	Thaw 1 hr at room temperature then whisk thoroughly.	Not recommended.	Defrost 12–15 min, per 600 ml (1 pint). Reheat as required.

CHAIN COOKING AND BATCH BAKING

Chain cooking and batch baking are easy methods of stocking the freezer with a variety of dishes without too much laborious preparation. Start with a large quantity of the same item such as minced beef, pastry or cake mixture, divide it into individual or family-size portions, then add different ingredients to each. Apart from the obvious economic advantage to be gained if you organize your shopping and preparation carefully, you can also cut down on the time and effort it would normally take to make so many different dishes.

Chain cooking comes into its own at many times throughout the year – before Christmas and holiday weekends, for example, before a big party or the children's school holidays. And at certain times of year when there is a glut of fruit and vegetables, chain cooking can also be used to avoid wastage, or to take advantage of seasonal bargains.

Decide what you are going to do before you start. Sit down and work out how much money you want to spend, how much freezer space you have to spare and how much time you can devote to preparation and cooking. Choose recipes that you know are popular with family and friends, and make out a careful shopping list for ingredients. Check that you have sufficient packaging materials such as foil, cling film, freezer bags and rigid containers, because you will need to put everything in the freezer as soon as it is cooked and cooled.

In this chapter, we have chosen to chain cook with two basic mixtures – minced beef and Victoria sandwich – but you can use virtually any ingredient you like. For example, stewing steak or chicken can be turned into casseroles, curries, goulash and pies, or bread dough can be made into loaves, rolls and pizzas. Look through your recipe books for inspiration.

CHAIN COOKING MINCED BEEF

Minced beef bought in bulk at the freezer food centre is less expensive than that bought loose by the kg/lb. Choose free-flow minced beef which can be cooked straight from the freezer. We have taken 2.5 kg/5 lb minced beef and turned it into 5 different dishes, each one serving 4–6.

To use your time and cooker space economically, it makes sense to start by cooking 1.5 kg/3 lb of the minced beef, then dividing it into Cottage Pie, Kheema Curry and Stuffed Peppers. While these are cooking you can make the remaining 1 kg/2 lb of beef into Italian Meatballs and Melting Meat Loaf. Of course, you don't have to stick rigidly to these suggestions.

Basic minced beef

1.5 kg/3 lb minced beef steak
3 tablespoons vegetable oil
2 large onions, finely chopped
3 garlic cloves, crushed
1×400 g/14 oz can tomatoes
2 tablespoons tomato purée
salt and black pepper

1 Heat the oil in a large, heavy-based saucepan, add the onions and garlic and fry gently for about 10 minutes until soft.
2 Add the beef a small quantity at a time and fry over gentle heat until browned. Stir constantly and press with the back of a spoon to remove any lumps before adding more.
3 Add the tomatoes, tomato purée and salt and pepper. Bring to the boil, stirring to break up the tomatoes, then simmer for 20 minutes.

Melting meat loaf and Stuffed peppers.

Kheema curry

Serves 4
⅓ quantity Basic minced beef
1 tablespoon vegetable oil
2.5 cm/1 inch piece root ginger
2 teaspoons ground coriander
1 teaspoon chili powder
1 teaspoon ground turmeric
100–175 g/4–6 oz frozen peas

1 Heat the oil in a heavy-based saucepan, add spices and fry gently for 5 minutes, stirring constantly.
2 Add the minced beef mixture and stir in the peas. Leave until cold.

To freeze
Pour into a rigid container, seal, label and freeze for up to 3 months.
To serve
Thaw in the container at room temperature for about 4 hours. Tip into a heavy-based saucepan and reheat until bubbling. Lower the heat, stir in about 150 ml/¼ pint yogurt and heat gently. Adjust the seasoning.

Cottage pie

Serves 4
⅓ quantity Basic minced beef
2 teaspoons grainy mustard
2 teaspoons demerara sugar
200 ml/7 fl. oz sweet stout
1 teaspoon dried mixed herbs
450 g/1 lb carrots, sliced
900 g/2 lb potatoes, peeled
salt and pepper
1 egg, beaten
25 g/1 oz butter

1 Boil the beef mixture until thick and stir in half the mustard with the sugar, stout and herbs.
2 Pour into a foil container or oven-proof dish lined with foil.
3 Boil the carrots and potatoes in salted water until tender, then mash. Add the remaining mustard, the egg and butter, and seasoning.
4 Spread the potato mixture over the beef. Mark with a fork. Cool.

To freeze
Open freeze solid. Cover foil container – or remove pie from dish and wrap in the foil – and freeze up to 3 months.
To serve
Uncover the container or unwrap the package and return pie to the original dish. Reheat in an oven preheated to 190°C/375°F/Gas Mark 5 for 1 hour.

Stuffed peppers

Serves 6
⅓ quantity Basic minced beef
3 medium red peppers
3 medium green peppers
50 g/2 oz cooked long-grain rice
50 g/2 oz seedless raisins
25 g/1 oz unsalted whole peanuts, shelled
2 tablespoons soy sauce
2 teaspoons soft brown sugar
1 tablespoon wine vinegar

1 Slice the tops off the peppers and carefully remove cores and seeds.
2 Blanch peppers and tops in boiling water for 5 minutes. Drain and rinse under cold running water. Pat dry.
3 Combine the remaining ingredients.
4 Stand the peppers upright in a rigid container. Divide the mixture between them, pressing it down well. Cover with tops and cool.

To freeze
Cover and freeze up to 3 months.

To serve
Thaw at room temperature for 6 hours. Cook in oven preheated to 180°C/350°F/Gas Mark 4 for 35–40 minutes.

Melting meat loaf

Serves 4
450 g/1 lb minced beef steak
1 tablespoon vegetable oil
1 onion, finely chopped
1 tablespoon tomato purée
225 g/8 oz pork sausagemeat
100 g/4 oz lean bacon, minced
50 g/2 oz fresh white breadcrumbs
2 eggs, beaten
1 tablespoon Worcestershire sauce
1 teaspoon dried mixed herbs
salt and black pepper
200 g/7 oz Mozzarella cheese, sliced

1 Heat the oil in a small pan, add the onion and tomato purée and fry gently for 5 minutes, stirring.
2 Mix the beef, sausagemeat, bacon and breadcrumbs in a bowl.
3 Add onion, eggs, sauce and herbs, and season. Mix to combine.
4 Place mixture on a sheet of foil about 45×30 cm/18×12 in and pat out to within 2.5 cm/1 in of the edge.
5 Arrange cheese over, leaving a margin around edge. Roll up meat like a Swiss roll. Place in the centre of the foil, join side down.

To freeze
Wrap the loaf tightly in the foil, seal, label and freeze for up to 3 months.
To serve
Reheat in an oven preheated to 190°C/375°F/Gas Mark 5 for 50 minutes. Open foil and place a few Mozzarella slices over the top. Bake for another 15 minutes.

Italian meatballs

Serves 6
450 g/1 lb minced beef steak
50 g/2 oz salami, finely chopped
50 g/2 oz fresh white breadcrumbs
1 egg, beaten
2 tablespoons chopped fresh parsley
¼ teaspoon freshly grated nutmeg
salt and black pepper
plain flour, for coating
vegetable oil, for frying
900 ml/1½ pints Fresh tomato sauce
  (see page 61)

1 Put all the ingredients (except the flour and oil) in a bowl and mix together until they are well combined.
2 Form the mixture into small balls, then coat in flour. Heat a little oil in a frying pan, add the balls a few at a time and fry over moderate heat until browned. Drain while frying the remainder, in more oil if necessary.
3 Add the meatballs to the Fresh tomato sauce. Stir to coat thoroughly and leave until cold.

To freeze
Pour the sauce and meatballs into a rigid container. Seal, label and freeze for up to 3 months.
To serve
Thaw in the container at room temperature for 4–6 hours. Tip into a heavy-based saucepan or casserole and reheat until bubbling, then taste and adjust seasoning.

This dish makes a robust main course accompanied by vegetables. Alternatively, serve as a sauce on freshly cooked pasta, sprinkled with 2 or 3 tablespoons of freshly grated Parmesan cheese.

BATCH BAKING WITH BASIC VICTORIA SANDWICH MIX

Baking cakes in batches saves time and fuel if they can be cooked in the oven at the same time, and there is nothing more convenient than having a cake or two tucked away.

The beauty of the basic Victoria sandwich mix is its versatility; it is also one of the quickest of cake mixtures to make, and it freezes well. From the four basic ingredients of sugar, butter, eggs and flour, you can make both plain, everyday cakes and special occasion gâteaux. You can follow the instructions given in the recipes on this page using butter or block margarine (butter has a far nicer flavour and better keeping qualities) or you can save time by using soft tub margarine and the all-in-one method of mixing. Almond Cherry Buns are plain everyday cakes; Chocolate Harlequin Cake is more suitable for a teatime treat; Orange and Walnut Liqueur Cake is a rather special recipe for a large gathering such as a coffee morning, and Lemon Cream Gâteau makes a luscious dinner party dessert.

To make things easy, weigh out all your ingredients first. Gather together all the correct cake tins and grease and line them as necessary. Check your oven size and shelf positions and decide which cakes can be cooked together – the oven temperature is the same in each of the recipes. If you have a double oven then so much the better, and if you have a large, table-top electric mixer you can save time by mixing more than one cake at one go.

For speed, we recommend mixing the four basic ingredients together for the Orange and Walnut Liqueur Cake and the Chocolate Harlequin Cake (ie 450 g [1 lb] each of butter, sugar and flour and 8 eggs), then dividing the mixture in half and adding the different flavouring ingredients as given in the recipes. The same can be done with the Lemon Cream Gâteau and Almond Cherry Buns. If you are short of freezer space, you can freeze the Orange and Walnut Liqueur Cake and the Lemon Cream Gâteau undecorated, then ice and fill them after thawing and before serving. Do not ice the Chocolate Harlequin Cake before freezing – glacé icing does not freeze successfully. Two final words of advice: when baking cakes for the freezer, use natural flavourings rather than artificial essences which tend to go 'musty' during storage; and be sure to freeze them as soon as possible after cooling, to preserve that 'just baked' flavour and freshness.

Almond cherry buns (page 45) and Harlequin cake.

Harlequin cake

Serves 8–10
225 g/8 oz butter or margarine
225 g/8 oz caster sugar
4 eggs, beaten
225 g/8 oz self-raising flour
¼ teaspoon salt
½ teaspoon vanilla flavouring
2 tablespoons cocoa powder
1 tablespoon black treacle
milk, to soften
To serve
2 teaspoons cocoa powder
1–2 tablespoons hot water
100 g/4 oz icing sugar
25 g/1 oz white chocolate, grated

1 Preheat the oven to 190°C/375°F/ Gas Mark 5.
2 Cream the fat and sugar until fluffy, then gradually beat in eggs.
3 Sift the flour and salt together, then gradually beat into the mixture.
4 Divide mixture in halves. Beat the vanilla into one, the cocoa and treacle into the other. Add milk to both if necessary, to soften to a dropping consistency.
5 Put alternate spoonfuls of mixtures in a 1.8 litre (3 pint) springform tin.
6 Bake in the oven for 30–35 minutes, until a skewer inserted into the cake comes out clean.
7 Cool in the tin for a few minutes, then turn out on a wire rack.

To freeze
Wrap the cake closely in cling film, then overwrap in foil or a bag. Seal, label and freeze for up to 10 months.
To serve
Thaw at room temperature for 4–6 hours. Dissolve the cocoa in a little of the hot water. Sift the icing sugar into a bowl, stir in the cocoa mixture, then gradually add enough hot water until the icing coats the back of a spoon. Drizzle over the cake and sprinkle with the chocolate.

Orange and walnut liqueur cake

Serves 8

225 g/8 oz butter or margarine
225 g/8 oz caster sugar
4 eggs, beaten
225 g/8 oz self-raising flour
¼ teaspoon salt
finely grated rind of 1 orange
2 tablespoons orange juice
1 tablespoon orange-flavoured
  liqueur
Buttercream icing
150 g/5 oz butter
350 g/12 oz icing sugar, sifted
finely grated rind of 1 orange
1 tablespoon orange juice
1 tablespoon orange-flavoured
  liqueur
orange food colouring
To serve
walnut halves
canned mandarin orange segments or
  crystallized orange slices

1 Preheat the oven to 190°C/375°F/
  Gas Mark 5. Grease two 20 cm/8
  inch sandwich tins, line the bases
  with greaseproof paper, then
  grease the paper.
2 Cream the fat and sugar together
  until light and fluffy, then beat in
  the eggs a little at a time.
3 Sift the flour and salt together, then
  beat into the creamed mixture a
  little at a time. Add the orange rind,
  juice and liqueur and beat again
  until evenly mixed.
4 Divide the mixture equally between
  the two sandwich tins and bake in
  the oven for 25 minutes, until well
  risen and firm to the touch.
5 Leave the cakes to cool in the tins
  for a few minutes, then turn out
  on to a wire rack. Leave until

completely cold.
6 Make the buttercream icing: cream
  the butter and icing sugar together
  until light and fluffy. Beat in the
  grated orange rind, orange juice
  and liqueur, then add a few drops
  of food colouring and beat until
  evenly mixed.
7 Sandwich the cakes together with
  some of the buttercream, then
  cover the sides and top of the cake
  with the remainder. Swirl with a
  palette knife to make an attractive
  pattern.

To freeze
Open freeze the cake until solid, then
pack carefully in a rigid container.
Seal, label and return to the freezer.
Store for up to 10 months.
To serve
Place the cake on a serving plate,
cover loosely with foil and leave to
thaw at room temperature for 4–6
hours. Decorate with walnut halves
and drained, canned mandarin orange
segments or crystallized orange slices
before serving.

Lemon cream gâteau

Serves 8–10

175 g/6 oz butter or margarine
175 g/6 oz caster sugar
3 eggs, beaten
175 g/6 oz self-raising flour
pinch of salt
finely grated rind of 1 lemon
juice of ½ lemon
milk, to soften
8 tablespoons lemon curd
300 ml/½ pint double cream, whipped to
  soft peaks
To serve
shreds of lemon rind

1 Preheat the oven to 190°C/375°F/ Gas Mark 5. Grease two 18 cm/7 inch sandwich tins; line the bases with greaseproof paper, then grease the paper.
2 Cream the fat and sugar together until light and fluffy, then beat in the eggs a little at a time.
3 Sift the flour and salt together, then beat into the creamed mixture a little at a time. Add the lemon rind and juice and beat again until evenly mixed. Add a few drops of milk if necessary, to soften to a dropping consistency.
4 Divide the mixture equally between the two sandwich tins and bake in the oven for 25 minutes, until well risen and firm to the touch.
5 Leave the cakes to cool in the tins for a few minutes, then turn out on to a wire rack. Leave until completely cold.
6 Split each cake in half. Place one round of cake on a board and spread with 2 tablespoons of the lemon curd. Spread a little cream over the curd, then place another round of cake on top.
7 Repeat with more lemon curd, cream and cake to make 4 layers of cake, 4 layers of lemon curd and 3 layers of cream.
8 Spread some of the remaining cream around the sides, then pipe the remainder around the top edge.

To freeze
Open freeze until solid, then pack carefully in a rigid container. Seal, label and return to the freezer. Store for up to 10 months.
To serve
Place the cake on a serving plate and leave to thaw in the refrigerator for 6–8 hours. Decorate before serving.

▌Almond cherry buns

Makes 15 buns
100 g/4 oz butter or margarine
100 g/4 oz caster sugar
2 eggs, beaten
100 g/4 oz self-raising flour
pinch of salt
50 g/2 oz glacé cherries, finely chopped
25 g/1 oz ground almonds
few drops of almond flavouring
about 2 tablespoons milk, to soften
To serve
icing sugar

1 Preheat the oven to 190°C/375°F/ Gas Mark 5.
2 Cream the fat and sugar together until light and fluffy, then beat in the eggs a little at a time.
3 Sift the flour and salt together, then beat into the creamed mixture a little at a time. Add the cherries, almonds and flavouring, and enough milk to soften to a dropping consistency.
4 Divide the mixture equally between 18 paper cake cases and stand them in bun or patty tins. Bake in the oven for 15–20 minutes, until well risen and firm to the touch.
5 Place the buns in their cases on a wire rack and leave until cold.

To freeze
Place the buns in rigid containers, separating the layers with foil or greaseproof paper. Seal and label, then freeze for up to 10 months.
To serve
Remove the buns from the containers and leave to thaw at room temperature for about 2 hours. Sift icing sugar over the tops of the buns just before serving.

COOKING FOR
THE FREEZER

Cooking dishes in advance is one of the best ways of making the most of your freezer. You can prepare ahead for a special occasion or simply cook double quantities when preparing an everyday meal. Special techniques like chain and batch cooking have already been described on pages 38 and 42; the recipes here are chosen to give you a good cross-section of ideas for all occasions, making use of a wide selection of ingredients covering starters, main courses and desserts. Useful standbys like stocks and sauces are included to help you build variety into your daily menu-planning. Don't be afraid to make use of ingredients from your freezer either as this can save valuable preparation time.

Watercress and broad bean soup

Serves 6
40 g/1½ oz butter or margarine
2 onions, chopped
1 tablespoon plain flour
1.2 litres/2 pints chicken stock
450 g/1 lb frozen broad beans
1 bouquet garni
225 g/8 oz watercress, trimmed
salt and pepper
To serve
2 egg yolks
150 ml/¼ pint double cream
croûtons, to garnish
thyme sprigs, to garnish

1 Melt the butter in a heavy-based saucepan, add the onions and cook for 5 minutes without browning. Add the flour and cook for 2 minutes, stirring constantly. Gradually stir in the stock, bring to the boil and simmer for 2 minutes.
2 Add the beans and bouquet garni. Return to boil, cover and simmer for 10 minutes, until tender.

3 Add the watercress and cook for a further 5 minutes. Season to taste.
4 Remove the bouquet garni, cool slightly, then purée. Cool completely.

To freeze
Pour into a rigid container, leaving 2 cm/¾ inch headspace, then seal, label and freeze for up to 6 months.
To serve
Thaw at room temperature for 3–4 hours. Pour into a saucepan and bring to the boil, stirring. Lower the heat. Blend yolks and cream smoothly, then stir in a little soup. Stir back into pan and heat through. Season and garnish.

Creamy carrot soup

Serves 4–6
50 g/2 oz butter or margarine
2 large onions, grated
2 garlic cloves, crushed
1 tablespoon plain flour
450 g/1 lb frozen carrots, thawed
salt and pepper
900 ml/1½ pints chicken stock

To serve
300 ml/½ pint double cream
4 tablespoons soured cream
1 carrot, grated

1 Melt the butter in a saucepan, add the onions and garlic and fry gently for 5 minutes without browning. Add the flour and cook for 2 minutes, stirring constantly.
2 Add the carrots and salt and pepper, then stir in the stock. Bring to the boil, stirring occasionally, then cover and simmer for 30 minutes, stirring from time to time.
3 Leave to cool slightly, then purée in a blender. Cool completely.

To freeze
Pour into a rigid container leaving 2 cm/¾ inch headspace, then seal, label and freeze for up to 4 months.
To serve
Reheat gently from frozen in a heavy-based saucepan, stirring frequently, then stir in the double cream. Pour into soup bowls, spoon the soured cream into the centre of each, then sprinkle with the grated carrot.

Watercress and broad bean soup and Creamy carrot soup.

■ Chicken liver pâté

Serves 4–6
50 g/2 oz butter or margarine
50 g/2 oz shallots, chopped
75 g/3 oz streaky bacon, rinds removed
  and chopped
450 g/1 lb frozen chicken livers
salt and pepper
pinch of ground nutmeg
1 tablespoon dry sherry
40 g/1½ oz butter or margarine, softened
squeeze of lemon juice
4 bay leaves
65 g/2½ oz butter

1 Melt the butter in a pan, add the shallots and bacon, then fry gently for 5 minutes. Add the chicken livers and fry them quickly over a high heat, stirring constantly until cooked and set.
2 Cool the mixture then purée in a blender or food processor. Beat in the salt and pepper, nutmeg, sherry, softened butter or margarine and the squeeze of lemon juice.
3 Spoon the mixture into a foil container, smoothing the surface. Place in the top of the refrigerator to set. Arrange the bay leaves on top of the mixture.
4 Melt 65 g/2½ oz butter in a pan, then leave to stand until the sediment settles to the bottom of the pan. Carefully pour the butter on to the top of the pâté. Set aside until the butter is cool and set to form a seal.

To freeze
Cover, label and freeze for up to 4 months.
To serve
Thaw in a cool place for 6 hours.

■ Kipper pâté with pimento

Serves 6
100 g/4 oz full fat soft cheese
225 g/8 oz frozen kipper fillets, thawed
1 tablespoon lemon juice
salt
paprika
2 tablespoons double cream
½ red pepper, cored, deseeded and finely
  chopped
To serve
4 lemon slices, twisted, to garnish

1 In a mixing bowl, cream the cheese with a wooden spoon until light and fluffy.
2 Cook the kipper fillets according to packet instructions. Drain and leave to cool slightly.
3 Skin and flake the kipper fillets, removing any small bones, then mash with a fork and beat into the cheese until well combined.
4 Add the lemon juice, salt and paprika to taste. Stir in the cream and red pepper.

To freeze
Place in a rigid container and smooth the surface. Seal, label and freeze for up to 2 months.
To serve
Thaw in the refrigerator for 6–8 hours. Transfer to a suitable serving dish or individual ramekin moulds and smooth the surface. Garnish with twisted lemon slices and serve with toast or slices of warm French bread.

Variations
This pâté can also be made with smoked mackerel or smoked trout and garnished with thin slices of cucumber as well as lemon slices.

Stuffed trout parcels

Serves 4
4 large frozen trout, thawed, heads and
backbones removed
For the stuffing
50 g/2 oz butter or margarine
175 g/6 oz frozen soft herring roes
1 tablespoon lemon juice
1 teaspoon creamed horseradish
1 tablespoon chopped parsley
salt and pepper
pinch of cayenne pepper
2 tablespoons fresh white breadcrumbs
To serve
Hollandaise sauce (see page 60)

1 Preheat the oven to 190°C/375°F/
  Gas Mark 5.
2 To make the stuffing, melt the
  butter in a saucepan, add the roes
  and fry gently for 5 minutes. Mash
  the roes with a fork and add the
  lemon juice, horseradish, parsley,
  salt and pepper and cayenne.
  Cook, stirring, for 2 minutes.
3 Remove from the heat and stir in
  the breadcrumbs. Set aside and
  allow to cool completely.
4 Butter 4 pieces of foil each large
  enough to enclose one trout. Divide
  the stuffing between the fish and
  place on a piece of foil. Wrap up to
  form secure parcels.

To freeze
Place the parcels in a polythene bag,
seal, label and freeze for up to 1
month.
To serve
Thaw at room temperature for 3–4
hours. Preheat the oven to 190°C/
375°F/Gas Mark 5. Bake the fish, in
the foil parcels, for 35 minutes.
Transfer to a warmed serving dish and
serve with Hollandaise sauce.

Stir-fried prawns

Serves 4
4 tablespoons oil
15 g/½ oz fresh root ginger, finely sliced
2 garlic cloves, crushed
8 spring onions, trimmed and sliced
1 medium carrot, peeled and cut into
matchstick strips
8 celery sticks, sliced diagonally
350 g/12 oz frozen cauliflower florets
225 g/8 oz frozen diced mixed peppers
225 g/8 oz frozen peeled prawns
celery leaves, to garnish
For the glaze
2 teaspoons cornflour
6 tablespoons water
2 teaspoons soy sauce
2 teaspoons tomato purée
salt and pepper

1 Heat the oil in a large frying pan,
  add the ginger and garlic and
  stir-fry over moderate heat for 30
  seconds.
2 Add the onions, carrot, celery and
  frozen cauliflower. Stir-fry for 2
  minutes. Add the peppers and stir-
  fry for another 1 minute, then add
  the prawns and heat until they are
  thawed and cooked through.
3 To make the glaze, mix together all
  the ingredients, then pour into the
  pan over brisk heat. Stir until the
  prawns and vegetables are well
  coated. Set aside to cool quickly.

To freeze
Pour the vegetables, prawns and glaze
into a rigid container, cover, label and
freeze for up to 1 month.
To serve
Reheat gently from frozen in a heavy-
based saucepan for 20–25 minutes,
stirring as necessary. Adjust seasoning
and serve garnished with celery.

North African lamb

Serves 4

1.25 kg/2½ lb frozen shoulder of lamb,
boned, rolled and tied and thawed
1 large aubergine, thickly cubed
1 garlic clove, crushed
a little olive oil (if necessary)
2 tablespoons Dijon-style mustard
2 tablespoons tomato purée
2 tablespoons wine vinegar
To serve
150 ml/¼ pint natural yogurt
mint sprigs, to garnish

1 Place the lamb in a dry, non-stick
   frying pan and brown on all sides.

2 Add aubergine and garlic. Fry for a
   few minutes, adding oil if necessary.

3 Mix togther the mustard, tomato
   purée and vinegar and make up to
   150 ml/¼ pint with water. Add to
   the pan, cover and simmer for 1 hour,
   or until the lamb is tender. Cool.

4 Remove the lamb from the sauce
   and slice thickly, discarding string.

To freeze
Overlap the slices in a 23 cm/9 inch
foil container and pour over sauce.
Seal, label and freeze up to 2 months.

Durham lamb chops (top) and North
African Lamb.

To serve
Thaw at room temperature for 4–5 hours. Loosen the lid, but do not remove, then reheat for about 50 minutes in an oven preheated to 160°C/325°F/Gas Mark 3, turning the slices over halfway through. Transfer to a warmed serving dish, swirl the yogurt over and garnish with mint.

Durham lamb chops

Serves 4

4 frozen chump lamb chops, thawed
2 tablespoons, plus 2 teaspoons flour
4 tablespoons oil
2 thick slices of bread, crusts removed and diced
2 onions, sliced
300 ml/½ pint milk
2 tablespoons chopped parsley
salt and pepper
To serve
parsley sprigs, to garnish

1 Coat the chops with 2 tablespoons of flour. Heat half the oil in a large frying pan, add the chops and fry over brisk heat until browned on both sides. Transfer the chops to an ovenproof dish lined with foil.
2 Add the bread cubes to the pan and fry gently, stirring, until evenly browned on all sides. Remove with a slotted spoon and drain on absorbent kitchen paper. Set aside.
3 Heat the remaining oil in the pan, add the onions and fry for 5 minutes, until soft but not brown.
4 Mix the remaining flour to a smooth paste with a little of the milk, then add remaining milk. Pour into the pan and bring to the boil, stirring constantly. Lower the heat and simmer for 2–3 minutes.

5 When the sauce has thickened, remove from the heat, stir in the parsley and season with salt and pepper. Pour over the chops, top with the bread cubes and set aside to cool.

To freeze
Open freeze the chops and sauce until solid, then remove from the dish in the foil and fold over the foil to make a parcel. Seal, label and freeze for up to 3 months.

To serve
Preheat the oven to 180°C/350°F/Gas Mark 4. Return to the original dish and open up the foil. Cook from frozen for 1 hour. Transfer the chops to a warmed serving dish and spoon over the sauce and bread cubes. Garnish with parsley sprigs and serve at once.

Normandy pork tenderloin (page 52).

Normandy pork tenderloin

Serves 4

25 g/1 oz can anchovy fillets, drained
14 almonds, shelled and peeled
7 prunes, pre-soaked and stoned
2 frozen pork tenderloins, thawed
50 g/2 oz butter or margarine
1 large onion, sliced
1 cooking apple, peeled, cored and
  thickly sliced
2 tablespoons demerara sugar
150 ml/¼ pint dry cider
150 ml/¼ pint white stock
1 teaspoon lemon juice
4 sage leaves, chopped
salt and pepper
1 tablespoon cornflour
2 tablespoons water
4 tablespoons double cream

1 Preheat the oven to 160°C/325°F/ Gas Mark 3.
2 Wrap each of the drained anchovy fillets around two of the shelled and peeled almonds and use these to stuff the prunes.
3 Slit each tenderloin lengthwise, cutting to within 1 cm/½ inch of the base, and open out. Place the stuffed prunes along the length of one fillet, then cover with the other. Tie the fillets together with kitchen string, tucking in the ends to make a neat shape.
4 Melt the butter in a flameproof casserole and brown the pork on all sides. Remove from the pan. Add the onion and apple to the pan. Sprinkle over the sugar, then pour in the cider, stock and lemon juice. Add chopped sage and the seasoning. Lay the pork over this mixture and cook in the oven for 40 minutes, or until tender.
5 Using a slotted spoon, remove the pork, then arrange the apple and onion in the bottom of a foil container. Lay the pork on top and remove the string.
6 Transfer the cooling juices to a saucepan and simmer for 5 minutes. Mix the cornflour with the water and stir into the sauce, then simmer for another 2–3 minutes. Remove from the heat and stir in the cream. Pour over the pork in the foil container. Set aside to allow to cool completely.

To freeze
Cover, label and freeze for up to 4 months.

To serve
Thaw overnight in the refrigerator. Preheat the oven to 160°C/325°F/Gas Mark 3. Loosen the lid and cook in the foil container for 35 minutes.

Variation
Flame the pork with 1 tablespoon of Calvados after browning it for an even more authentic flavour of the cuisine of Normandy.

Beef Oxford

Serves 4

1 kg/2 lb frozen cubed stewing steak
40 g/1½ oz plain flour
50 g/2 oz dripping
salt and pepper
2 large onion, sliced
2 garlic cloves, crushed
100 g/4 oz mushrooms, trimmed
  and sliced
75 g/3 oz frozen diced mixed peppers
2 tablespoons apricot jam
300 ml/½ pint red wine
300 ml/½ pint beef stock

1 Place the beef in a polythene bag with the flour and shake until well coated.

2 Melt the dripping in a large flameproof casserole and fry the meat over brisk heat, until browned on all sides. Add all the remaining ingredients, including any flour left over in the bag, bring to the boil, then cover and simmer for 2–2½ hours, or until the meat is tender, stirring occasionally.

To freeze
Transfer to a rigid container, cool, cover, label and freeze for up to 3 months.

To serve
Thaw overnight in the refrigerator. Place in a large saucepan over moderate heat and reheat gently, stirring, until piping hot. Transfer to a warmed serving dish and serve at once with baked potatoes.

Variation
This quick-and-easy casserole can also be made with diced pork, substituting white stock for the beef stock.

Stuffed rump steak

Serves 6

850 g/1¾ lb frozen rump steak 2.5 cm/
1 inch thick, thawed
100 g/4 oz thinly sliced raw smoked ham
15 g/½ oz butter or margarine
75 g/3 oz button mushrooms, trimmed
and quartered
1 tablespoon finely chopped parsley
or coriander
salt and pepper
1 tablespoon oil
1 tablespoon soured cream
4 tablespoons red wine
½ teaspoon paprika

1 Cut the flesh of the steak to form a pocket. Overlap half the ham slices in the bottom of the pocket.

2 Melt the butter in a frying pan, add 50 g/2 oz of the mushrooms and fry gently for a few minutes. Remove from the heat and stir in the parsley and pepper to taste. Spread over the ham and top with the remaining ham.

3 Close the pocket and secure with wooden cocktail sticks.

4 Heat the oil in a frying pan, add the meat and fry over brisk heat for 3 minutes on each side. Remove from the pan and sprinkle with salt and pepper. Pad the ends of the cocktail sticks with foil, then place in an ovenproof dish lined with foil.

5 Add the cream and wine to the pan and stir to dissolve the sediment. Add the paprika and the remaining mushrooms, cook for 2 minutes, then pour over the steak. Set aside to cool quickly.

To freeze
Open freeze until solid. Remove the steak from the dish in the foil and fold over the edges to make a secure parcel. Seal, label and return to the freezer for up to 2 months.

To serve
Unwrap and return to the original dish. Cover with foil and thaw at room temperature overnight. Preheat the oven to 200°C/400°F/Gas Mark 6 and cook for 20–25 minutes. Remove the cocktail sticks and serve sliced thickly.

Variation
A similar technique can be used with several different stuffings for the steak. Try sliced salami, seedless raisins and sage, or liver pâté, breadcrumbs and brandy.

Malayan chicken curry

Serves 4

50 g/2 oz butter or margarine
1 kg/2¼ lb frozen chicken portions,
  thawed
2 Spanish onions, sliced
1 tablespoon plain flour
1 tablespoon curry paste
450 ml/¾ pint milk
4 tablespoons lemon juice
1 tablespoon peach chutney
75 g/3 oz salted peanuts
salt and pepper
1 tablespoon cornflour
4 tablespoons water

1 Melt the butter in a large heavy-based saucepan, add the chicken joints and brown them on all sides. Remove the chicken and set aside.
2 Add the onions to the pan and fry for 6–8 minutes, until light golden. Stir in the flour and curry paste and cook for another 1–2 minutes. Stir in the milk, lemon juice, chutney, peanuts and salt and pepper. Bring to the boil, stirring constantly.
3 Add the chicken, cover and simmer for 30–40 minutes.
4 Remove the chicken and arrange in a foil container. Mix together the cornflour and water and stir into the sauce. Bring to the boil and simmer for 2–3 minutes, stirring constantly. Pour over chicken. Cool.

To freeze
Cover, label and freeze for up to 3 months.
To serve
Thaw for 3–4 hours at room temperature. Preheat the oven to 160°C/325°F/Gas Mark 3. Loosen the container lid and cook for 35–40 minutes. Serve on a bed of brown rice.

Malayan chicken curry.

Chicken and prawn pilaf

Serves 6

350 g/12 oz cooked long-grain rice
50 g/2 oz butter or margarine
1 Spanish onion, sliced
100 g/4 oz frozen diced mixed peppers
1 garlic clove, crushed
1 teaspoon turmeric
1 teaspoon dried oregano
75 g/3 oz button mushrooms, sliced
50 g/2 oz shelled unsalted peanuts
200 g/7 oz can red kidney beans, drained
  and rinsed in cold water
2 tablespoons chopped parsley
225 g/8 oz frozen peeled prawns
450 g/1 lb cooked chicken, chopped
salt and pepper
50 g/2 oz Parmesan cheese, grated

Chicken and prawn pilaf.

1 Heat the butter in a large flame-proof casserole and add the onion, peppers and garlic. Fry gently for 6−8 minutes until onion is golden.
2 Stir in the turmeric, oregano, mushrooms, peanuts, beans and parsley, then cook for another 2−3 minutes. Add the prawns and chicken and stir-fry for 5−7 minutes. Season and fold in rice.
3 Place in a large foil container and sprinkle the cheese over the top. Allow to cool completely.

To freeze
Cover, label and freeze up to 3 months.
To serve
Thaw at room temperature for 6 hours. Preheat oven to 160°C/325°F/Gas Mark 3 and cook for 30−40 minutes.

Cherry duckling

Serves 4
2¼ kg/5 lb frozen duckling, thawed
salt
For the cherry sauce
1 Spanish onion, chopped
150 ml/¼ pint red wine
450 ml/¾ pint chicken stock
3 tablespoons cornflour
6 tablespoons water
425 g/15 oz frozen black cherries
salt and pepper

1 Preheat the oven to 200°C/400°F/Gas Mark 6.
2 Prick the duckling skin all over with a fork and sprinkle over salt. Place on a wire tray in a roasting tin and cook for 45 minutes. Turn over and cook for another 45 minutes.
3 Cover with foil to prevent over-browning. Return to its original position and cook for 30 minutes, until juices run clear. Cool slightly.
4 Divide the duckling into 4 joints, then place in a large foil container.
5 Place 2 tablespoons of the duckling fat in a pan. Add onion and fry for about 5 minutes until soft. Pour in the wine and stock. Boil until reduced to about 450 ml/¾ pint.
6 Mix the cornflour with the water and stir into the sauce. Simmer for 2−3 minutes, stirring constantly, then add the cherries and seasoning and heat through. Pour over the duckling. Cool.

To freeze
Cover, and freeze for up to 4 months.
To serve
Thaw at room temperature for 4−5 hours. Preheat oven to 160°C/325°F/Gas Mark 3, loosen lid and cook 35−40 minutes, basting with sauce.

Crème brûlée with grapes

Serves 6
175 g/6 oz white grapes, halved and pips
removed
6 egg yolks
2 tablespoons caster sugar
600 ml/1 pint double cream
1 vanilla pod
4 tablespoons demerara sugar, to serve

1 Preheat the oven to 120°C/250°F/ Gas Mark ½.
2 Arrange the grapes in the base of a 900 ml/1½ pint ovenproof dish. Cream together the egg yolks and caster sugar until pale.
3 Gently heat the double cream with the vanilla pod until the cream is tepid, remove the pod and pour the cream on to the egg yolk mixture. Blend together, then strain over the grapes.
4 Place the dish in a roasting tin half filled with boiling water. Cook the brûlée for 1 hour, or until the custard is set. Set aside to cool.

To freeze
Place in a polythene bag, seal, label and freeze for up to 4 months.
To serve
Remove from the polythene bag and sprinkle the demerara sugar evenly over the top. Preheat the grill to high, then place the dish under the grill until the sugar melts. Stand at room temperature for 2 hours before serving.

Variations
Other fruits, such as strawberries, raspberries, chopped apricots or cherries, can be used instead of the halved white grapes.

Lemon cheesecake

Serves 6
50 g/2 oz butter or margarine
25 g/1 oz demerara sugar
100 g/4 oz digestive biscuits, crushed
225 g/8 oz full fat soft cheese
150 ml/¼ pint double cream
200 g/7 oz can condensed milk
4 tablespoons lemon juice
To serve
4 tablespoons double cream, whipped
6 lemon slices, twisted

1 Melt the butter in a saucepan, then mix in the sugar and biscuit.
2 Press mixture into sides and base of a deep 18 cm/7 inch flan dish.
3 Beat the cream cheese until soft. Whisk in the cream and milk, then slowly whisk in the lemon juice.
4 Pour the mixture into the crumb case and smooth the surface.

To freeze
Cover with foil. Freeze up to 6 weeks.
To serve
Thaw overnight at room temperature. Decorate with cream and lemon slices.

Meringue glacé

Serves 8
½ litre/1 pint raspberry ripple ice cream
red food colouring
For the meringues
3 egg whites
175 g/6 oz caster sugar
For the filling
250 ml/8 fl oz double cream
1 tablespoon icing sugar, sifted
175 g/6 oz frozen raspberries
To serve
3 tablespoons double cream, whipped
8 frozen raspberries, thawed

1 Line 3 baking sheets with greaseproof paper. With a pencil, draw three 15 cm/6 inch circles on the paper.
2 To make the meringues, preheat the oven to 120°C/250°F/Gas Mark ½. Whisk the egg whites until stiff, then whisk in 3 tablespoons of the sugar. Fold in the remaining sugar with a large metal spoon.
3 Spoon into a piping bag fitted with a 1 cm/½ inch plain nozzle and pipe in to the circles marked on the paper. Bake for 2 hours, or until very crisp. Carefully peel the paper off the meringues, then place on a wire rack to cool.
4 To make the filling, whip the cream with the icing sugar until it will stand in soft peaks, then fold in the raspberries.
5 Mix the slightly softened ice cream with a little red food colouring until it is well blended and a pleasing raspberry pink colour.
6 Line the bottom and sides of a 20 cm/8 inch cake tin with a layer of raspberry ice cream. Place a meringue round on top and cover with half the raspberry filling. Repeat these layers and top with the third round, filling any spaces on the sides with ice cream.

To freeze
Cover with foil, wrap in a polythene bag, seal, label and freeze for up to 3 months.
To serve
Unwrap and invert on to a serving dish. Rub the tin with a cloth wrung out in very hot water until the cake drops out. Decorate with piped cream and raspberries, then transfer to the refrigerator 1 hour before serving to soften. Serve chilled.

Variation
For a more varied dessert, use strawberry ice cream to line the sides and bottom of the tin and use a combination of whole raspberries and strawberries to decorate the top.

Chocolate and cherry bombe

Serves 6–8
½ litre/1 pint chocolate ice cream
For the filling
225 g/8 oz frozen black cherries, quartered
2 tablespoons kirsch
1 tablespoon caster sugar
225 ml/8 fl oz double cream
To serve
4 tablespoons double cream, whipped

1 To make the filling, place the cherries in a bowl with the kirsch and sugar and leave for 1 hour.
2 Whip the cream until it stands in stiff peaks, then fold in the cherries and kirsch.
3 Line a chilled 1.5 litre/2½ pint bombe mould or freezerproof basin thickly with chocolate ice cream softened enough to mould.
4 Fill the centre with the cherry filling.

To freeze
Cover the bombe mould with its lid or cover the basin with foil, then wrap in a polythene bag. Seal, label and freeze for up to 3 months.
To serve
Unwrap the mould and invert on to a serving dish. Rub with a cloth wrung out in very hot water until the bombe drops out. Decorate with piped whipped cream, then transfer to the refrigerator for 30 minutes to soften.

Strawberry cream sponge

Serves 8
3 eggs
150 g/5 oz caster sugar
75 g/3 oz plain flour, sifted
1 tablespoon oil
To serve
150 ml/¼ pint double cream, whipped
225 g/8 oz strawberries, sliced
icing sugar, to dust

1 Preheat the oven to 190°C/375°F/ Gas Mark 5. Grease a deep 20 cm/ 8 inch cake tin, line the base with greaseproof paper, then grease the paper. Dust the inside of the tin lightly with flour.
2 Place the eggs and sugar in a bowl and whisk until thick and the batter holds the impression of the beater when the beaters are lifted.
3 Turn the batter into the tin and level the surface. Bake for 20–25 minutes, until the cake springs back when lightly pressed in the centre. Turn out on to a wire rack, peel off the paper, turn the cake right way up and cool.

To freeze
Open freeze, pack in a bag, seal, label and freeze for up to 10 months.
To serve
Unwrap and thaw at room temperature for 2–3 hours. Cut the cake into 2 layers. Place the bottom half on a serving dish and spread with the cream. Cover with strawberries. Place the remaining layer on top and sift the icing sugar over the top. Serve the same day.

Variations
For a banana cream cake, dip 225 g/ 8 oz banana slices in lemon juice and place on top of the cream, then sprinkle 50 g/2 oz shredded coconut over the bananas. Assemble as above. Raspberries or poached apple slices can also be substituted for the strawberries.

Peach gâteau

Serves 8
3 eggs, separated
100 g/4 oz caster sugar
finely grated rind of ½ lemon
2 tablespoons lemon juice
50 g/2 oz semolina
25 g/1 oz ground almonds
To serve
4 thinly sliced frozen peaches, thawed
300 ml/½ pint double cream, whipped
4 tablespoons apricot jam
2 teaspoons lemon juice
50 g/2 oz flaked almonds, toasted

1 Preheat the oven to 180°C/350°F/ Gas Mark 4. Grease a deep 20 cm/ 8 inch cake tin, line the base with greaseproof paper, then grease the paper. Dust the inside of the tin lightly with flour.
2 Place the egg yolks, sugar, lemon rind and lemon juice in a bowl and whisk until the batter is thick and holds the impression of the beaters when they are lifted.
3 Stir in the semolina and ground almonds. Whisk the egg whites until stiff, then fold in.
4 Pour the batter into the prepared tin and level the surface. Bake for 35–40 minutes, until the cake springs back when lightly pressed in the centre. Turn out on to a wire rack, peel off the lining paper, turn the cake the right way up and leave to cool.

To freeze
Open freeze, wrap in a bag, seal, label and freeze for up to 10 months.
To serve
Unwrap and thaw at room temperature for 2–3 hours, then cut into 2 layers. Fold half the peach slices into three-quarters of the cream and use to sandwich the two layers. Heat the jam and lemon juice gently,

Strawberry cream sponge and Peach gâteau.

stirring, until the jam has melted. Sieve and reheat. Arrange the remaining peach slices overlapping in a circle on top of the cake. Brush the warm glaze over the sides and top of cake, then press nuts around sides. Pipe remaining cream around top.

Beef stock

Makes about 600 ml/1 pint
1 kg/2 lb marrow and shin bones
½ teaspoon salt
1 onion, quartered
2 carrots, peeled and chopped
1 bouquet garni
6 black peppercorns

1 Place the bones in a large saucepan. Cover with 2 litres/3½ pints water and add the salt. Bring to the boil, skimming off any scum with a slotted spoon, half cover and simmer for about 2 hours, skimming occasionally.
2 Add the remaining ingredients and continue to simmer for another 1½–2 hours, adding more water as necessary.
3 Strain into a clean pan and set aside to cool, then skim off any remaining fat with a spoon or absorbent kitchen paper.

To freeze
Boil rapidly until the stock is reduced to one-third of its original volume. Place in ice cube trays or small freezerproof containers and freeze for up to 2 months.
To use
Add the concentrated stock cubes to water that is two-thirds the amount of stock required by the recipe. Boil the water and cubes together, stirring, until the stock dissolves.

Variations
For chicken stock, use a whole chicken carcass rather than beef bones. Duck and turkey stock can be made in the same way.
For white stock, use blanched veal bones.

Hollandaise sauce

Makes about 250 ml/8 fl oz
1 tablespoon cornflour
3 tablespoons water
3 egg yolks
2 tablespoons lemon juice
225 g/8 oz butter, melted and cooled
salt and freshly ground black pepper

1 Blend the cornflour and water in a small pan. Boil and whisk until a thick transparent paste. Cool.
2 Over a low heat, whisk the yolks and lemon juice in a heavy saucepan until just thickening.
3 Pour into a blender and turn on. Add the butter in a thin stream until the sauce is the consistency of thick cream. Season and mix in cornflour.

To freeze
Pour into a rigid container, cover, label and freeze for up to 4 months.
To serve
Thaw at room temperature for 5–6 hours. Stand in a bowl of warm water and stir constantly to warm through.

Sweet and sour sauce

Makes about 300 ml/½ pint
1 tablespoon oil
1 onion, diced
150 ml/¼ pint dry white wine
1 tablespoon wine vinegar
1 tablespoon peach chutney
1 tablespoon tomato ketchup
1 teaspoon soy sauce
1 teaspoon prepared mustard
salt and pepper
pinch of mixed spice
pinch of chili powder
1 tablespoon cornflour
6 tablespoons water

1 Heat the oil in a saucepan and gently fry the onion for about 5 minutes, until soft. Pour in the wine, and boil for 2 minutes
2 Add the vinegar, chutney, tomato ketchup, soy sauce, mustard, salt and pepper, mixed spice and chili. Cover and simmer for 20 minutes.
3 Cool slightly, then sieve or blend in blender, and return to the pan.
4 Blend the cornflour with the water and stir into the sauce. Re-boil and simmer for 2–3 minutes. Cool.

To freeze
Pour into a rigid container, cover, label and freeze for up to 4 months.
To serve
Place in a saucepan over low heat until thawed. Bring to boil, stirring.

Fresh tomato sauce

Makes about 900 ml/1½ pints
3 tablespoons oil
2 Spanish onions, finely diced
2 garlic cloves, crushed
5 tablespoons tomato purée
450 g/1 lb tomatoes, skinned and chopped
pinch of sugar
1 teaspoon Worcestershire sauce
2 bay leaves
rosemary sprig
salt and pepper
250 ml/8 fl oz dry white wine
1 tablespoon cornflour
2 tablespoons water

1 Heat the oil in a saucepan and gently fry the onions and garlic for 8–10 minutes. Stir in the tomato purée, tomatoes, sugar, Worcestershire sauce, bay leaves, the rosemary sprig and seasoning.

2 Pour in the wine and bring the sauce to the boil. Cover and simmer for about 40 minutes. Blend the cornflour with the water and add to the sauce. Simmer for another 5 minutes. Set aside to cool.

To freeze
Remove the bay leaves and rosemary, then pour into a rigid container, or freeze in half quantities for use as topping on frozen pizza bases. Cover, label and freeze for up to 4 months
To serve
Place in a pan over low heat until thawed, then bring to the boil.

Melba sauce

Makes about 300 ml/½ pint
350 g/12 oz frozen raspberries
150 ml/¼ pint water
1 tablespoon caster sugar
1 tablespoon arrowroot
1 tablespoon redcurrant jelly
1 tablespoon orange juice
1 tablespoon gin

1 Place the raspberries, water and sugar in a saucepan and bring to the boil. Purée in a blender or sieve, then return to the saucepan.
2 Stir in the arrowroot, redcurrant jelly and orange juice and bring back to the boil. Cook for 3 minutes. If liquidized, strain the sauce into a bowl. Stir in the gin, then set aside to cool.

To freeze
Pour into a rigid container, cover, label and freeze for up to 4 months.
To serve
Thaw at room temperature for 6 hours.

COOKING FROM
THE FREEZER

A well-stocked freezer is a boon for the busy but adventurous cook. It ensures you a wide selection of vegetables, fruit, meat, poultry and fish, whatever the season, and you can also freeze so many of those little extras that make a dish exciting: double cream for soups and desserts; herbs – especially parsley – frozen chopped in convenient quantities in individual ice-making trays; basics like onion rings, sliced peppers and grated cheese frozen 'free-flow' so you can use a little at a time. Many ingredients can be used straight from the freezer without thawing if needed in small quantities, and you can save hours of preparation time by stocking frozen pastry and ready-made flan cases or sponge rings.

Smoked fish soup

Serves 4

600 ml/1 pint milk
1 kg/2 lb frozen smoked haddock
225 g/8 oz potatoes, peeled and diced
2 onions, chopped
parsley sprig
salt and pepper
lemon juice
40 g/1½ oz butter, diced
150 ml/¼ pint single cream
cayenne pepper, to garnish

1 Place the milk and fish in a pan and slowly bring to the boil. Cover and simmer for 5 minutes.
2 Strain, reserving the liquid. Flake the fish, removing any bones.
3 Bring the liquid to the boil, then add potatoes, onions and parsley. Season and simmer for 20 minutes.
4 Add the fish and cook for 10 minutes. Remove parsley and add lemon juice to taste. Gradually stir in the butter, then the cream.
5 Ladle the soup into warmed bowls, sprinkle cayenne over and serve.

Hungarian broth

Serves 6

15 g/½ oz lard
1 onion, chopped
1 carrot, peeled and chopped
625 g/1¼ lb frozen boneless diced pork
1 small white cabbage, shredded
600 ml/1 pint frozen meat stock, thawed
dash of vinegar
1 teaspoon paprika
salt and pepper
1 teaspoon cornflour
2 teaspoons water
120 ml/4 fl oz soured cream
chopped parsley, to serve

1 Melt the lard in a flameproof casserole, add the onion and carrot and cook gently for 6 minutes.
2 Add the pork, cabbage and stock, cover and simmer for 30 minutes.
3 Stir in vinegar, paprika and season. Blend the cornflour and water to a smooth paste and add to the broth with the cream. Simmer for 2 minutes, stirring constantly.
4 Sprinkle with parsley to serve.

French onion quiche

Serves 6

225 g/8 oz frozen shortcrust pastry, thawed
2 Spanish onions, sliced
3 eggs
250 ml/8 fl oz frozen double cream, thawed
salt and pepper
pinch of paprika
50 g/2 oz grated Gruyère cheese

1 Preheat the oven to 200°C/400°F/ Gas Mark 6.
2 Roll out the pastry on a lightly floured surface and use to line a 20 cm/8 inch flan case. Line with greaseproof paper and weight down with baking beans. Bake for 15 minutes, then remove the beans and paper and bake for another 5 minutes. Allow to cool slightly on a wire rack.

3 Reduce the oven temperature to 190°C/375°F/Gas Mark 5.
4 Put the onions in a pan of boiling salted water and simmer for 5 minutes. Drain.
5 Arrange the onions in the flan case.
6 Beat together the eggs, cream, salt and pepper and paprika, then pour over onion. Sprinkle cheese over.
7 Bake for 25–30 minutes, until the filling is set and top is golden brown. Serve warm or chilled.

Variation
Quiche Lorraine can be made by substituting 6 rashers of streaky bacon for the onions; remove the rinds and chop the bacon, then fry the bacon in a dry frying pan until the fat runs. Drain and place in the bottom of the flan case. Proceed as above.

Broccoli in puff pastry (page 64) and Smoked fish soup.

Broccoli in puff pastry

Serves 6–8
400 g/14 oz frozen broccoli spears
600 ml/1 pint frozen chicken stock,
  thawed
15 g/½ oz butter or margarine
100 g/4 oz cooked ham, chopped
salt and pepper
215 g/7½ oz packet frozen puff pastry,
  thawed
2 eggs, beaten
1 tablespoon chopped parsley
1 egg yolk

1 Preheat the oven to 220°C/425°F/
  Gas Mark 7.
2 Place the broccoli in a saucepan
  with the stock and bring to the boil.
  Lower the heat and cook for 8–10
  minutes, until tender.
3 Meanwhile, melt the butter in a
  frying pan and quickly fry the ham.
  Drain. Chop the broccoli and add to
  the ham with seasoning.
4 Roll out the puff pastry on a lightly
  floured surface to a 25 cm/10 in
  square. Spoon the broccoli and
  ham mixture into the centre of the
  pastry, then carefully pour the
  beaten eggs over the mixture.
  Sprinkle with the parsley and adjust
  the seasoning if desired.
5 Fold the corners of the pastry into
  the centre and pinch and firmly seal
  the edges together. Brush with egg
  yolk and place on a dampened
  baking sheet.
6 Bake for 25–30 minutes until the
  filling is set and the pastry golden.

Variation
For a vegetarian meal, replace the
ham with 175 g/6 oz frozen
sweetcorn. Do not fry; simply add to
the chopped broccoli.

Stuffed plaice in prawn sauce

Serves 4
4 frozen plaice fillets, thawed
For the stuffing
50 g/2 oz fresh white breadcrumbs
2 tablespoons chopped fresh parsley
75 g/3 oz grated Gouda cheese
1 tablespoon lemon juice
2 tablespoons single cream
1 egg yolk
salt and pepper
For the sauce
150 ml/¼ pint milk
25 g/1 oz butter or margarine
2 tablespoons plain flour
1 tablespoon cornflour
2 tablespoons water
75 g/3 oz frozen peeled prawns, thawed
salt and pepper
150 ml/¼ pint single cream
lemon twists, to garnish

1 Preheat the oven to 160°C/325°F/
  Gas Mark 3. Butter an ovenproof
  serving dish.
2 Lay the fillets flat on a board. Mix
  together all the stuffing ingredients
  and divide equally between the
  fillets. Roll up each fillet to enclose
  the stuffing.
3 Place the fish rolls in the prepared
  serving dish, then pour in the milk.
  Cover the dish with foil and bake
  for 20 minutes.
4 Using a slotted spoon, remove the
  fish and set aside to keep warm.
  Reserve the cooking liquid.
5 Melt the butter in a saucepan and
  stir in the flour. Cook for 2–3
  minutes, then gradually stir in the
  reserved liquid. Bring to the boil.
6 Blend the cornflour with the water
  and stir into the sauce. Continue
  simmering for 3–4 minutes.

7 Stir in the prawns, salt and pepper and then the cream. Spoon over the fish and garnish with lemon slices. Serve at once on a bed of boiled rice mixed with chopped fresh dill.

Variation
This quick and easy sauce can also be used over frozen fillets of sole that have been thawed and poached in a court bouillon of water or milk with a little lemon juice.

Salmon surprise

Serves 6
2 large frozen salmon steaks weighing
  450 g/1 lb, thawed and skinned
2 onions, sliced
6 black peppercorns
1 lemon slice
salt
50 g/2 oz long-grain rice
25 g/1 oz butter or margarine
175 g/6 oz frozen sliced mushrooms
50 g/2 oz grated Gruyère cheese
1 tablespoon lemon juice
175 ml/6 fl oz single cream
pinch of ground nutmeg
salt and pepper
1 tablespoon cornflour
2 tablespoons water
2 tablespoons chopped fresh parsley
375 g/13 oz packet frozen puff pastry,
  thawed
2 eggs, beaten

1 Place the salmon in a pan with the onions, peppercorns, lemon slice and salt and sufficient water to cover. Cover the pan and bring the contents slowly to the boil.
2 Remove from the heat and set aside for 10 minutes. Strain and reserve liquid. Bone and flake the salmon.

3 Cook the rice in an equal volume of the reserved liquid until just tender, then strain and cool.
4 Preheat the oven to 190°C/375°F/Gas Mark 5.
5 Melt the butter in a small saucepan and gently fry the mushrooms for 2–3 minutes. Stir in the cheese, lemon juice, cream, nutmeg and salt and pepper. Cook gently until the cheese has melted and all the ingredients are well blended.
6 Mix the cornflour with the water and stir into the sauce. Simmer for 2–3 minutes, stir in parsley and cool.
7 Roll out the pastry to a 36 cm/14 inch square. Spread half the rice over the pastry to form a 18 cm/7 inch square in the centre. Spoon half the sauce over that. Arrange the salmon over the sauce and spoon remaining sauce over. Cover with remaining rice.
8 Draw up the two sides of the pastry to overlap by 25 cm/1 inch and seal with beaten egg. Trim away the pastry from each end to within 25 cm/1 inch of the filling. Seal with beaten egg and crimp the edges.
9 Cut a 5 cm/2 inch wide strip of pastry from the trimmings, and place over the join, sealing with beaten egg. Make pastry leaves from the remaining trimmings and use to decorate the top.
10 Bake for 25 minutes, then reduce the heat to 160°C/325°F/Gas Mark 3 and continue cooking for 25 minutes. Serve sliced hot or chilled.

Variation
A more economical version of this recipe can be made with cod or smoked haddock. For special occasions, serve with thawed Hollandaise sauce (see page 60).

Salmon surprise (page 65).

Prawns Provençale

Serves 4–6
1 tablespoon oil
2 onions, chopped
1 garlic clove, crushed
*400 g/14 oz tomatoes, peeled, deseeded
  and chopped*
175 g/6 oz frozen mixed diced peppers
3 tablespoons dry white wine
1 tablespoon chopped fresh parsley
1 tablespoon chopped fresh oregano
1 tablespoon chopped fresh basil
dash of Tabasco sauce
1 teaspoon Worcestershire sauce
salt and pepper
1 tablespoon tomato purée
350 g/12 oz frozen prawns, thawed
basil leaves, to garnish

1 Heat the oil in a large frying pan,
   add the onions and garlic and fry
   gently until soft but not coloured.

2 Add tomatoes, peppers and wine
   and bring to the boil, then reduce the
   heat and add the herbs, sauces and
   seasoning. Simmer, uncovered, for
   40 minutes, until reduced and thick.
3 Increase the heat and boil rapidly
   for another 5 minutes. Reduce heat
   and stir in purée and prawns.
   Simmer gently for 5 minutes.
4 Transfer to a heated serving dish
   and garnish with basil leaves. Serve
   with boiled rice and hot garlic bread.

Summer beef casserole

Serves 6
25 g/1 oz butter or margarine
2 tablespoons oil
1 kg/2 lb frozen boneless diced beef steak
175 g/6 oz frozen peeled baby onions
225 g/8 oz frozen baby carrots
1 tablespoon plain flour
1 tablespoon tomato purée
450 ml/¾ pint frozen beef stock, thawed
1 bay leaf
parsley sprig
marjoram sprig
salt and pepper
175 g/6 oz frozen French beans
175 g/6 oz frozen sliced courgettes
75 g/3 oz frozen mushrooms
To serve
4 tablespoons double cream
½ teaspoon paprika

1 Preheat the oven to 160°C/325°F/
   Gas Mark 3.
2 Melt the butter and oil in a large
   frying pan, and quickly brown the
   beef cubes. Transfer the meat to a
   large heatproof casserole.
3 Add the onions and carrots to the
   pan and stir-fry to brown lightly.
4 Stir in the flour and tomato purée,
   then gradually add the stock.

5 Add the herbs and salt and pepper and pour over the beef.
6 Cover the casserole and cook for 1¼–1½ hours. Add the beans, continue cooking for another 30 minutes. Spoon cream over the top and sprinkle with the paprika.

Beef goulash

Serves 6

3 tablespoons oil
1 kg/2 lb frozen boneless diced beef steak
2 Spanish onions, sliced
175 g/6 oz frozen mixed diced peppers
2 tablespoons paprika
400 g/14 oz can tomatoes
300 ml/½ pint frozen beef stock, thawed
1 teaspoon dried thyme
1 teaspoon dried marjoram
salt and pepper
3 tablespoons cornflour
175 ml/6 fl oz plain yogurt

1 Preheat the oven to 180°C/350°F/ Gas Mark 4.
2 Heat the oil in a large frying pan and quickly brown the meat. Transfer the meat to a large heatproof casserole.
3 Add the onions and peppers and fry until softened and lightly browned.
4 Add the paprika and cook for a further 2–3 minutes. Stir in the tomatoes, stock, herbs and salt and pepper. Pour over the meat.
5 Cover and cook for 2 hours.
6 Blend the cornflour with all but 2 tablespoons of the yogurt, then stir into the dish and return to oven for 5 minutes. Trickle remaining yogurt over the top to serve.

Summer beef casserole (top) and Beef goulash.

Spicy lamb chops

Serves 4
2 tablespoons oil
4 frozen lamb chump chops
1 Spanish onion, sliced
75 g/3 oz frozen mixed diced peppers
1 teaspoon ground cumin
1 teaspoon chili powder
1 tablespoon apricot jam
1 teaspoon tomato purée
1 teaspoon Worcestershire sauce
1 tablespoon wine vinegar
300 ml/½ pint frozen chicken stock,
  thawed
4 tomatoes, skinned, deseeded and
  chopped
50 g/2 oz salted peanuts
salt and pepper
1 tablespoon cornflour
2 tablespoons water

1 Preheat the oven to 160°C/325°F/
   Gas Mark 3.
2 Heat the oil in a large frying pan
   and quickly fry the chops on both
   sides until thawed and browned.
   Transfer to a large casserole.
3 Fry the onion and peppers until
   lightly browned. Add the cumin
   and chili powder and stir-fry over a
   high heat for 2–3 minutes.
4 Lower the heat, add the apricot
   jam, tomato purée, Worcestershire
   sauce, vinegar, stock, tomatoes and
   peanuts to the pan, then bring to
   boil. Season and pour over chops.
5 Cover and bake for 40 minutes.
6 Remove the chops from the
   casserole and set aside to keep
   warm. Mix the cornflour and water
   together and add to the sauce.
   Cook over moderate heat, stirring,
   until thickened. Return the chops to
   the casserole, cook a further 1
   minute. Serve at once.

Irish stew

Serves 4–6
50 g/2 oz dripping
1 kg/2 lb frozen lamb chops
2 onions, sliced
600 ml/1 pint frozen chicken stock,
  thawed
1 bouquet garni
salt and pepper
2 tablespoons pearl barley
450 g/1 lb potatoes, peeled and cubed
1 tablespoon fresh chopped parsley

1 Allow the lamb to thaw at room
   temperature.
2 Preheat the oven to 160°C/325°F/
   Gas Mark 3.
3 Heat the dripping in a large frying
   pan and quickly fry the lamb on
   all sides until fully sealed and
   browned. Remove from the pan
   and place in a large heatproof
   casserole.
4 Fry the onions until lightly
   browned, then add to the meat.
5 Pour the stock into the casserole,
   then add the bouquet garni, salt
   and pepper and sprinkle the barley
   over.
6 Cover and bake for 1½ hours,
   stirring occasionally. Add the
   potatoes and continue cooking for
   another 30–40 minutes, until the
   meat is tender and the potatoes are
   cooked through. Stir in the parsley,
   being careful not to break up the
   potatoes. Serve at once with Garlic
   beans or Crunchy cauliflower (see
   page 72).

Variations
For an Irish beef stew, substitute
frozen boneless diced beef for
the lamb and beef stock for the
chicken stock.

Pork chops with apples

Serves 4
2 tablespoons oil
4 frozen pork chops
225 g/8 oz frozen baby onions
1 garlic clove, crushed
100 g/4 oz frozen apple slices
salt and pepper
300 ml/½ pint cider
4 tablespoons double or soured cream
parsley sprigs, to garnish

1 Heat the oil in a large frying pan and quickly fry the chops until thawed and browned on both sides, adding a little more oil if necessary. Remove from the pan and keep warm.
2 Add the frozen onions and garlic to pan and fry for about 5 minutes, until the onions are thawed and soft.
3 Return the chops to the pan and lay the apple slices on top. Season and pour on the cider. Cover and simmer gently for 30 minutes.
4 Stir in the cream, being careful not to break up the apples, and serve at once garnished with the parsley sprigs, with frozen carrots, steamed and mixed with butter and finely chopped fresh mint.

Variations
For special occasions 1 tablespoon Calvados, a French apple-flavoured brandy, can be added to the pan with the cider.
  This dish works equally with frozen diced pork. Serve it on a bed of hot buttered noodles or fluffy white rice with some seedless raisins forked through it.

Kidneys turbigo

Serves 4
25 g/1 oz butter or margarine
1 tablespoon oil
225 g/8 oz frozen cocktail sausages
12 frozen lambs' kidneys, halved
150 g/5 oz frozen baby onions
100 g/4 oz frozen sliced mushrooms
300 ml/½ pint beef stock
2 tablespoons Madeira or port wine
1 tablespoon cornflour
3 tablespoons water
1 tablespoon chopped fresh parsley
salt and pepper
To serve
croûtons
parsley sprigs

1 Melt the butter and oil in a large frying pan and fry the sausages and kidneys until the kidneys are thawed and all the meat is browned on all sides. Remove from the pan and keep warm.
2 Add the onions to the pan and fry for about 5 minutes, until thawed and soft, then add the mushrooms and cook for 2 minutes.
3 Make a Demi-glace sauce: in a small pan bring the stock and Madeira or port to the boil. Blend cornflour and water to a smooth paste, stir in a little hot stock and return to the pan. Simmer gently until thickened, stirring constantly.
4 Return the kidneys and sausages to the frying pan and pour over the Demi-glace sauce.
5 Cover and simmer for 25 minutes, stirring occasionally. Stir in the chopped parsley and adjust the seasoning if necessary. Serve garnished with croûtons and parsley sprigs. Serve with creamed potatoes or boiled rice.

69

Chicken with olives.

Chicken with olives

Serves 4
50 g/2 oz butter or margarine
75 g/3 oz back bacon, cut into strips
100 g/4 oz frozen sliced mushrooms
25 g/1 oz plain flour
250 ml/8 fl oz frozen chicken stock,
  thawed
salt and pepper
750 g/1½ lb frozen boneless chicken
  breasts, cooked and diced
75 g/3 oz stuffed olives, sliced
250 ml/8 fl oz frozen double cream
1 tablespoon cornflour
2 tablespoons water

1 Preheat the oven to 160°C/325°F/
  Gas Mark 3.
2 Melt the butter in a large frying pan
  and fry the bacon gently for 4–5
  minutes. Add mushrooms and cook
  for 2–3 minutes, stirring.

3 Stir in the flour and cook until the
  mixture is well blended. Pour in the
  stock, season and bring to boil.
4 Lower the heat, then stir in the
  chicken, olives and frozen cream.
  Mix the cornflour and water
  together and stir into the sauce.
  Cook, stirring constantly, for 2–3
  minutes, until the sauce thickens.
  Serve at once on a bed of rice with
  mixed frozen vegetables, steamed
  and tossed in butter.

Variation
This can be made with leftover
chicken, or even leftover lamb.

Baked Parmesan chicken

Serves 4
8 frozen chicken portions, thawed
seasoned flour, for coating
100 g/4 oz fresh white breadcrumbs
50 g/2 oz Parmesan cheese, grated
2 tablespoons chopped fresh parsley
1 egg, beaten
150 g/5 oz butter or margarine
1 garlic clove, crushed
parsley sprigs, to garnish

1 Preheat the oven to 200°C/400°F/
  Gas Mark 6. Grease a roasting tin.
2 Place the chicken pieces and
  seasoned flour into a polythene bag
  and shake until the chicken is well
  coated.
3 Mix together the breadcrumbs,
  Parmesan cheese and parsley.
4 Dip the chicken pieces, one by one,
  into the beaten egg, then into the
  breadcrumb mixture.
5 Arrange the chicken pieces in the
  roasting tin and bake for 10–15
  minutes.

6 Meanwhile, melt the butter in a saucepan and stir in the garlic. Pour over the chicken, making sure all the pieces are well basted.

7 Reduce the oven temperature and continue cooking for another 30 minutes. Garnish with parsley sprigs and serve with crisp bacon rolls and oven baked chips.

Tarragon chicken

Serves 6

75g/3 oz butter or margarine
1 tablespoon oil
6 frozen boneless chicken breasts, thawed
2 tablespoons chopped fresh tarragon
salt and pepper
600 ml/1 pint frozen chicken stock,
  thawed
2 tablespoons cornflour
4 tablespoons water
250 ml/8 fl oz frozen double cream
fresh tarragon sprigs, to garnish

Baked Parmesan chicken (left) and Tarragon chicken.

1 Preheat the oven to 180°C/350°F/ Gas Mark 5.

2 Melt the butter and oil in a large frying pan, add the chicken and fry gently until browned on both sides.

3 Transfer the chicken and pan juices to a heatproof casserole and add the tarragon, stock and seasoning.

4 Cover and cook for 30 minutes.

5 Transfer the chicken to a serving dish and keep warm.

6 Mix the cornflour and water together, then stir into the cooking liquid. Simmer 2–3 minutes, stirring, until the sauce thickens. Then stir in the frozen cream, portion by portion until it has dissolved. Adjust the seasoning, if necessary, and pour the sauce over the chicken. Garnish with fresh parsley sprigs and serve at once with frozen petits pois.

French beans with bacon and tomato

Serves 6
750 g/1½ lb frozen French beans
6 rashers streaky bacon, rinds removed and cut into strips
3 large tomatoes, skinned, deseeded and cut into strips
1 teaspoon caster sugar
salt and pepper
1 tablespoon chopped fresh parsley, to garnish

1 Cook the beans in boiling salted water until just tender. Drain and cut into 5 cm/2 inch lengths.
2 Place the bacon in a dry frying pan and fry for about 4 minutes, until fat begins to run. Stir in the tomatoes, sugar and salt and pepper.
3 Add the beans to the tomato mixture and cook for about 6 minutes, stirring occasionally. Place the beans on a warmed serving dish, garnish with the parsley and serve at once.

Variation
For a sharper tasting dish, add 1 crushed garlic clove to the bacon fat before adding the other ingredients and add 50 g/2 oz frozen mixed diced peppers with the tomatoes. Proceed as above and garnish with strips of chopped stoned black olives.

Garlic beans

Serves 6
450 g/1 lb frozen French beans
25 g/1 oz butter or margarine
2 tablespoons oil
2 garlic cloves, crushed
pepper

1 Cook the beans in boiling salted water until just tender. Drain and set aside.
2 Meanwhile, melt the butter and oil together in a saucepan and add the crushed garlic. Toss the beans in the garlic butter and season to taste with pepper. Serve hot or chilled as a salad.

Crunchy cauliflower

Serves 6
450 g/1 lb frozen cauliflower florets
4 rashers streaky bacon, rinds removed
50 g/2 oz fresh white breadcrumbs
1 hard-boiled egg, halved
pepper

1 Cook the cauliflower in boiling salted water until just tender. Drain and arrange in a flameproof serving dish and set aside to keep warm.
2 Place the bacon in a dry frying pan and fry for about 4 minutes, until crispy. Drain on absorbent paper, then crumble the bacon into a bowl.
3 Fry the breadcrumbs in the bacon fat until crispy, drain and add to the bacon.
4 Sieve the egg yolk into the breadcrumb mixture. Finely chop and add the egg white, and mix all the ingredients together. Season with pepper.
5 Preheat the grill to high.
6 Sprinkle the topping over the florets and put the dish under the grill for 1 minute to heat through. Serve at once.

Variation
Frozen broccoli spears are also delicious prepared with the above topping.

Vegetable lasagne

Serves 6

4 tablespoons olive oil
3 large onions, sliced
2 garlic cloves, crushed
450 g/1 lb tomatoes, skinned, deseeded
  and chopped
150 ml/¼ pint dry white wine
2 teaspoons chopped fresh basil
2 teaspoons chopped fresh parsley
2 teaspoons chopped fresh oregano
salt and pepper
1 tablespoon tomato purée
350 g/12 oz frozen sliced courgettes
225 g/8 oz frozen broad beans
100 g/4 oz frozen peas
450 g/1 lb spinach or egg lasagne

For the sauce

600 ml/1 pint milk
2 carrots, peeled and chopped
1 small onion, chopped
1 leek, trimmed and chopped
1 bay leaf
few peppercorns
50 g/2 oz butter or margarine
50 g/2 oz plain flour
2 teaspoons Dijon-style mustard
175 g/6 oz Cheddar cheese, grated
50 g/2 oz Gruyère cheese, grated
1 tablespoon freshly grated Parmesan
  cheese
parsley sprigs, to garnish

1 Heat half the oil in a large
   saucepan, add the onions and garlic
   and fry gently for 7–8 minutes,
   until lightly browned. Add the
   skinned, deseeded and chopped
   tomatoes and the wine, bring to
   the boil, then simmer uncovered for
   20 minutes.

2 Add the chopped fresh basil,
   parsley and oregano and salt and
   pepper to taste and continue
   cooking for another 5 minutes.

3 Stir in the tomato purée,
   courgettes, broad beans and peas
   and continue cooking for 5 minutes
   until the vegetables are cooked
   through. Remove from the heat.

4 To make the sauce, put the milk,
   carrots, onion, leek, bay leaf and
   salt and peppercorns into a
   saucepan. Bring to the boil, remove
   from the heat, cover and leave to
   infuse until cold. Strain and reserve
   the milk.

5 Melt the butter in the rinsed-out
   pan, add the flour and cook for
   2 minutes, stirring constantly.
   Remove from the heat and
   gradually stir in the flavoured milk,
   whisking well after each addition.
   Return to the heat and slowly bring
   to the boil.

6 Lower the heat and add the
   mustard and cheeses and simmer,
   stirring constantly, until the cheeses
   are melted. Taste and adjust the
   seasoning.

7 Meanwhile, bring a large pan of
   salted water to the boil with the
   remaining olive oil. Cook the
   lasagne in batches according to the
   packet instructions. Drain, cool
   under cold running water and drain
   again thoroughly.

8 Preheat the oven to 200°C/400°F/
   Gas Mark 6. Lightly grease an
   ovenproof dish.

9 Arrange a layer of pasta in the base
   of the dish. Spoon over some of the
   vegetables, then top with another
   layer of pasta and cover with a layer
   of cheese sauce. Continue until all
   the ingredients are used, finishing
   with a layer of sauce.

10 Bake for 40 minutes, until bubbling
   and golden on top. Serve at once,
   garnished with parsley, with slices
   of French bread.

Blackberry parfait

Serves 4–6

450 g/1 lb frozen blackberries with stalks removed
4 tablespoons water
2 teaspoons lemon juice
50 g/2 oz sugar
2 egg whites
75 g/3 oz caster sugar
300 ml/½ pint frozen double cream, thawed

1 Place the blackberries in a saucepan with the water, lemon juice and sugar and simmer for about 15 minutes, until the berries have softened.
2 Work the cooled berries to a purée in an electric blender, then press through a fine sieve to remove the pips.
3 Pour into a rigid container, cover and freeze for 2–3 hours, until half frozen. Remove from the freezer and transfer to a bowl. Whisk thoroughly to remove all the ice crystals.
4 Whisk the egg whites until stiff, then whisk in the sugar, 1 tablespoon at a time. Continue whisking until the meringue is very stiff.
5 Whip the cream until it stands in soft peaks, then fold into the meringue with the blackberry mixture. Spoon into chilled glasses and serve at once with crisp rolled biscuits.

Variation

You can also make this impressive-looking dessert with other frozen fruits, such as strawberries and raspberries or a combination of any red summer fruits.

Strawberry ice cream with Melba sauce

Serves 6

450 g/1 lb frozen strawberries, thawed
225 g/8 oz icing sugar, sifted
300 ml/½ pint frozen double cream, thawed and lightly whipped
300 ml/½ pint frozen Melba sauce, thawed (see page 61)

1 Work the strawberries to a purée in an electric blender, then sieve into a large mixing bowl.
2 Gradually stir the icing sugar into the purée, then fold in the cream.
3 Transfer the mixture to ice trays without the dividers and freeze for at least 2–3 hours. Scoop into bowls and spoon over sauce.

Boston raspberry tart

Serves 6

225 g/8 oz frozen shortcrust pastry, thawed
plain flour, for dusting
225 g/8 oz frozen raspberries
1 tablespoon ground cinnamon
225 g/8 oz caster sugar
4 tablespoons redcurrant jelly

1 Roll out the pastry on a lightly floured surface and use to line an 18 cm/7 in flan dish, reserving the trimmings. Chill until ready to fill.
2 Place the raspberries in a saucepan with the cinnamon and sugar and cook gently for 15–20 minutes. Cool.
3 Preheat the oven to 190°C/375°F/ Gas Mark 5.
4 Fill the flan with the raspberries. Re-roll trimmings and make a lattice top for the tart.

5 Bake for 25–30 minutes, then set aside to cool. Melt the jelly and brush over the top to form a glaze. Serve chilled with vanilla ice cream.

Baked Alaska

Serves 6

one 20 cm/8 in frozen uniced Victoria
  sponge, thawed
4 tablespoons sweet sherry
225 g/8 oz frozen sliced nectarines or
  peaches, thawed
For the meringue
4 egg whites
250 g/8 oz caster sugar
½ litre/1 pint vanilla ice cream

Baked Alaska.

1 Place the sponge on a heatproof serving dish and sprinkle over sherry. Arrange the fruit over.
2 To make the meringue: whisk the egg whites until stiff, then gradually whisk in sugar. Set aside.
3 Preheat the oven to 230°C/425°F/ Gas Mark 7.
4 Soften the ice cream slightly, then shape it into a dome over the fruit slices, leaving a 2.5 cm/1 inch margin all round. Quickly spoon the meringue over the ice cream and sponge to cover them completely.
5 Bake for 8–10 minutes until lightly browned. Serve immediately.

INSTANT
TAKEAWAYS

'Takeaway' meals may be convenient but they are often dull, poorly cooked or expensive. With your freezer, you can have all the takeaways you could want for a fraction of the cost, with more quality and variety. With a stock of frozen chips, fish in batter, burgers and buns, ice cream, ready-made pizzas or pizza bases, even frozen curries and kebabs, you can have all the regular 'Takeaways' at your finger tips – and you don't even have to leave home! With a few extra ingredients, the recipes suggest ways you can add a delicious home-cooked touch to any instant meal, whether a quick snack after a night out, an impromptu party or when you're just too busy to cook for yourself or the family.

Instant pizza party

Serves 4
4×50 g/2 oz frozen basic pizza bases
450 ml/¾ pint frozen fresh Tomato sauce
  (see page 61)
Alternative toppings
100 g/4 oz frozen sliced mushrooms
225 g/8 oz frozen mixed diced
  peppers
2 finely chopped onions
1 frozen deseeded and chopped chili
100 g/4 oz cooked sausagemeat,
  crumbled
100 g/4 oz finely diced ham
225 g/8 oz grated hard cheese

1 Preheat the oven to the required temperature given with the pizza bases.
2 Place the frozen sauce in a saucepan over low heat until thawed, then bring to the boil.
3 Place the pizza bases on a baking sheet and spoon the fresh tomato sauce equally over the top of each. Arrange the desired toppings and sprinkle the cheese over the tops.

4 Bake according to the instructions with the pizza bases, until the pizza and toppings are cooked through. Serve with a mixed salad.

Variations
The above suggested toppings can also be used to liven up frozen prepared pizzas that already have a simple topping.

Cheesy bacon-burger platters

Serves 4
4 streaky bacon rashers, rinds removed
4 frozen beefburgers
4 frozen burger rolls
350 g/12 oz frozen battered onion rings
100 g/4 oz grated Cheddar or Cheshire
  cheese
4 lettuce leaves
2 medium tomatoes, sliced
To serve
mustard
ketchup
mayonnaise

1 Preheat the grill to moderate. Grill the bacon until crispy, then set aside to drain on absorbent kitchen paper. Keep warm.
2 Grill or fry the beefburgers, according to the packet instructions. Thaw the rolls briefly under the grill to crisp them.
3 Meanwhile, fry or bake the onion rings according to packet instructions.
4 When the beefburgers are cooked, crumble a bacon rasher over the top of each and top with grated cheese. Return to the grill until the cheese is melted and bubbling and slightly browned.
5 Assemble the cheesy bacon-burgers on the buns and top each burger with a lettuce leaf and tomato slices. Serve with the onion rings and a selection of condiments listed above.

Variations

Sliced onions and mushrooms and finely chopped red or green peppers are ideal beefburger toppings. If frozen, thaw for 1–2 hours at room temperature, then use instead of bacon. Oven baked chips are a good alternative to the onion rings that can also be cooked from frozen.
For a really authentic touch of the American-style hamburger restaurant supply bowls of chopped raw onion and various pickles and relishes.
For a light meal, prepare the beefburgers and serve with thawed and reheated Sweet and sour sauce (see page 60) or Fresh tomato sauce (see page 61) spooned over them. Accompany with potato croquettes and broccoli spears or cauliflower florets cooked straight from the freezer and lightly buttered.

Sweet and sour spring rolls

Serves 4

½ pint frozen Sweet and sour sauce (see page 60)
8 frozen spring rolls, thawed
225 g/8 oz cooked hot rice

1 Place the sweet and sour sauce in a saucepan over low heat until thawed. Bring to the boil, stirring rapidly, until smooth. Set aside to keep warm.
2 Meanwhile, prepare the spring rolls according to the packet instructions.
3 Serve the spring rolls on a bed of hot rice with the sweet and sour sauce spooned over the top. Serve with stir-fried Chinese vegetables and meat.

Variation

A good way to use up leftover rice is to make Chinese fried rice to serve with the spring rolls. Heat 6 tablespoons oil in a wok or large frying pan and quickly cook 1 finely chopped onion and 1 crushed garlic clove for about 5 minutes, until the onion is soft. Add 400 g/14 oz thawed prawns and cook, stirring for 2 minutes, then add 350 g/12 oz diced cooked ham and 350 g/12 oz diced cooked pork along with 225 g/8 oz leftover rice for 5 more minutes, stirring constantly. Add soy sauce to taste and season with salt and pepper. Serve with the spring rolls, sweet and sour sauce and stir-fried Chinese vegetables and meat.
For a more substantial meal include 2 × 350 g/12 oz packets of frozen Spare ribs in barbecue sauce, cooked according to packet instructions.

Stir-fried Chinese vegetables and meat

Serves 4

2×350 g/12 oz frozen Oriental-style mixed vegetables
225 g/8 oz rump or braising steak frozen in matchstick-sized pieces
3 tablespoons oil
fresh chopped ginger, to taste
100 g/4 oz beansprouts
soy sauce, to taste

1 Let the meat thaw briefly in the refrigerator until the pieces separate.
2 Heat 1 tablespoon oil in a large frying pan and add the chopped ginger, stirring until the ginger starts to brown and flavours the oil.
3 Add the meat and stir until it is almost cooked through.
4 Add 1–2 tablespoons oil, if necessary, and the vegetables. Stir-fry according to the packet instructions. One minute before the end of the recommended cooking time add the beansprouts and continue stirring. Season to taste with soy sauce. Serve at once with sweet and sour spring rolls and rice.

Variations

Matchstick-sized pieces of pork, lamb and chicken can also be used.
For a quick-and-easy French-style meal, make the above recipe with Mediterranean-style mixed vegetables, omitting the beansprouts and replacing the ginger with a crushed garlic clove. Serve with hot garlic bread; if using frozen garlic bread, thaw at room temperature for 3–4 hours then heat through in an oven preheated to 200°C/400°F/Gas Mark 6 for 12–15 minutes.

Southern-style meal in a basket

Serves 4

8 frozen crispy coated chicken portions and nibbles
750 g/1½ lb frozen chips
For sweetcorn fritters
100 g/4 oz plain flour
pinch of salt
1 egg, beaten
150 ml/¼ pint milk
350 g/12 oz frozen sweetcorn
oil, for frying

1 Preheat the oven according to the packet instructions for the crispy chicken portions.
2 Place the chicken pieces on a baking sheet and bake according to the instructions.

3 Cook the chips according to the packet instructions, draining on absorbent kitchen paper if fried; set aside to keep warm.

4 Meanwhile, to make the sweetcorn fritters, sift the flour and salt into a large mixing bowl. Make a well in the centre and add the beaten egg, then gradually whisk in half the milk, drawing in flour from the sides.

5 Whisk vigorously until smooth, then pour in the remaining milk and whisk to remove all lumps. Mix in the sweetcorn and season to taste.

6 Heat two tablespoons of oil in a large frying pan. Add a few spoonfuls of the batter, leaving space between, and fry for 2–3 minutes on each side until golden brown. Drain on absorbent paper and set aside to keep warm.

Stir-fried Chinese vegetables and meat (left) and Southern-style meal in a basket.

7 Line 4 round bread baskets or bowls with folded sheets of absorbent paper and fill with the chicken portions, chips and sweetcorn fritters.

Variations
The chips can be replaced with frozen potato croquettes or frozen onion rings, prepared according to the packet instructions. Hot herby bread and coleslaw also go well with this type of meal.

For a light evening meal, serve the crispy chicken with thawed and reheated Fresh tomato sauce (see page 61) and a mixed green salad.

INDEX

ACKNOWLEDGMENTS
Photographers: Paul Williams,
Robert Golden
Stylists: Penny Markham,
Antonia Gaunt
Home economists: Caroline
Ellwood, Heather Lambert